PLANT-BASED
SLOW COOKER
COOKBOOK

PLANT-BASED SLOW COOKER COOKBOOK

100 Whole-Food Recipes Made Simple

FELICIA SLATTERY

PHOTOGRAPHY BY LAURA FLIPPEN

ROCKRIDGE
PRESS

Interior and Cover Designer: Lisa Forde

Art Producer: Sara Feinstein

Editor: Gleni Bartels

Production Editor: Rachel Taenzler

Production Manager: Holly Haydash

Photography © 2021 Laura Flippen. Food styling by Laura Flippen. Illustrations used under license from Shutterstock.com. Author photo courtesy of Lori Santoro Photography.

ISBN: Print 978-1-64876-601-5 | eBook 978-1-64739-595-7

R0

I dedicate this book to the memory of my father and my grandparents, as well as to my mother, who all were my first teachers in the kitchen.

CONTENTS

Introduction
viii

CHAPTER ONE

**Plant-Based Cooking,
Deliciously Slow**
1

CHAPTER TWO

Breakfasts
17

CHAPTER THREE

**Snacks and
Appetizers**
29

CHAPTER FOUR

Sides
45

CHAPTER FIVE

**Soups, Stews,
and Chilis**
59

CHAPTER SIX

Entrées
93

CHAPTER SEVEN

Desserts
119

CHAPTER EIGHT

**Basics and
Bonus Recipes**
133

Quick Reference Cooking Guide
152

**Measurement
Conversions**
154

**Resources and
References**
155

Index
156

INTRODUCTION

In 2012, at age 42, I was diagnosed with lung cancer. Because I didn't have any health or environmental red flags, my doctors shrugged their shoulders and said, "We'll never know why this happened to you." That was not a good enough explanation.

I always thought I was a healthy eater. Long ago I had given up things like artificial colors and flavors, started growing my own veggies and herbs, and started eating free-range eggs and "clean" meats and cheeses—but I discovered that my diet could be the root cause of my illness. After being cured from cancer, I dove into various diets and food plans, including eating gluten-free, juicing, counting calories, dabbling with paleo, and ultimately eating a meat-, dairy-, and egg-heavy keto diet. Following keto, I lost more than 30 pounds, but over time my normally healthy cholesterol skyrocketed and much of the weight came back. My doctor suggested I try eating a plant-based diet for a month to see how my body responded.

I was well prepared to take on the new challenge, thanks to my lifelong love of food and years studying cooking methods. My love of food began in my grandparents' kitchen as I watched my grandfather (a first-generation Italian American with his own butcher shop) make magic for Sunday suppers. It evolved through my taking nutrition class in high school, attending cooking classes in Paris when I studied abroad in college, and becoming a food blogger to chronicle my recipes. As I studied the plant-based way of eating, I decided to pursue a plant-based nutrition certification to learn more. I discovered that countless doctors and researchers have shown that eating plant-based food is best for the human body. Eating plant-based is also better for the environment, is a more sustainable way to eat, and is friendly to animals.

As a busy home-based business owner, author, and mother, I long ago fell in love with my slow cooker. But I'll admit that after beginning to eat a plant-based diet, my slow cooker began gathering dust. I couldn't quite figure out how (or why) to use it for my new way of life. But then I realized that, with some tweaking, many of my favorite recipes like stews and soups—and even my award-winning chili recipe (page 90)—lent themselves to being prepared in a slow cooker. I dusted it off and have never looked back!

Golden Split
Pea Soup,
Page 67

Rosemary-and-Garlic
Beet Salad with
Walnuts and Dijon-
Maple Dressing,
Page 46

In this book, just like on my website and Facebook group PlantBasedHomeCooking.com (and on my YouTube channel with the same name), you'll find recipes for delicious, fuss-free, mostly hands-off dishes, with no more than 20 minutes of prep time—yay! You'll find recipes inspired by a variety of cuisines from around the world as well as many regional influences from across the United States, all of which are suitable for every type of plant-based diet.

Thank you for joining me. I'm excited for you to discover the joys of plant-based home cooking in your slow cooker.

CHAPTER ONE

Plant-Based Cooking, Deliciously Slow

Before we start cooking, let's look at the fundamentals of both plant-based eating and slow cooking. I'll give an overview of three of the most common plant-based diets and the ingredients you'll see throughout these recipes. I'll talk about the kinds of slow cookers available today, offer some technique tips, and show you how to think about using your slow cooker in a way you may not have considered before. Then I'll give some information about the book itself, so you can easily find the recipes that will fit your personal needs and learn how to make them work best for you.

WHAT DOES "PLANT-BASED" MEAN, ANYWAY?

The benefits of a plant-based diet are numerous. Thousands of research studies performed over decades have shown that eating plant-based food is great for the human body. It has been shown to prevent, treat, and even reverse numerous life-threatening diseases such as heart disease, some cancers, diabetes, and autoimmune disorders, as well as stave off cognitive conditions such as Alzheimer's. Eating a plant-based diet can also lead to weight loss, and environmentally speaking, it's a more sustainable way to eat and is animal friendly.

A quick search will show you that people interpret "plant-based" in varied ways, and pinning it down is trickier than it sounds. Add to that the confusion over what makes something "plant-based" versus "vegan," and you've got a real challenge not just with semantics but also with what to eat! I want to clarify, too, that when I use the word "diet," I'm not referring to a crash diet, a fad diet, or any other short-term change to the way you eat in order to lose a few pounds. The intention of a plant-based diet is a long-term lifestyle change that allows you to enjoy the many benefits of a diet free of animal products. No matter the plant-based diet you follow, you'll be able to adapt these recipes to fit your guidelines.

Plant-Based

A standard plant-based diet is rich in fruits, vegetables, tubers (like potatoes), whole grains, legumes, nuts, and seeds. It also permits various flours, sugars, and other sweeteners, plant-derived protein powders, and plant-derived oils such as olive, avocado, or coconut. Since this definition of the diet allows for meat and dairy alternatives and faux meat products, I've offered them as additions to recipes where I think they'd really take things up a notch, like Green Pepper, Potato, and Mushroom Scallopini Sandwiches (page 108) and Mushroom Stroganoff (page 104). There is no plant food that is off-limits on a standard plant-based diet; however, it is not necessarily meant for—or best for—weight loss, if that is your goal.

How is this different from "vegan"? Many who identify as vegan practice the philosophy of "do no harm." Therefore, in addition to removing animal products from their diets, vegans also don't use any animal by-products, such as leather or fur clothing and accessories.

Whole-Food, Plant-Based (WFPB)

In addition to all of the fruits, veggies, and legumes mentioned earlier, a whole-food, plant-based diet emphasizes eating foods that are as close as possible to how they were grown—unrefined or minimally refined. For a WFPB diet, the less processing the plant-based ingredient has undergone, the better, which means recipes favor whole-wheat flour over white flour (even unbleached), brown rice over white rice, and products like whole-grain breads, pastas, and tortillas. In this eating plan, sugar, oil, and salt are acceptable in moderation, and throughout this book, you'll see these as suggested or optional ingredients.

Whole-Food, Plant-Based, and SOS-Free (WFPBSOS)

This diet is about what *isn't* included: Salt, Oil, or refined Sugar—that's the "SOS" part. Even oils that have been considered "healthier," like olive and avocado, are not part of this diet. That is why all of the recipes in this book will have any salt and oils as optional ingredients—and will be just as delicious without them. Sweeteners in the WFPBSOS diet include maple syrup or dried fruits, such as dates, blended with water to form a paste or liquid (see page 134), but none of these recipes use refined sugars.

You might think that eating this way will be bland, but when you use a full range of flavorful seasonings, herbs, and spices, your palette adjusts to taste the natural sweet or salty flavors in plant-based foods. If your goal is to lose weight or dramatically decrease your likelihood of experiencing a multitude of common health challenges, the WFPBSOS diet has been called the gold standard of plant-based diets and can help you achieve these goals.

SLOW COOKER BASICS

I love a slow cooker. I'm a busy mom and business owner, and as I get started with my work for the day, I love the feeling of having the ingredients for dinner—or breakfast or lunch—already in the slow cooker, bubbling away as I go about whatever is on my proverbial plate. Haven't thought about pulling out your slow cooker in a while? Here are some reasons to reach for it.

Super easy prep and cleanup: Chop a few ingredients, open a can or two, season it up, and you're good to go. One-pot cooking? Yes, please! (Try the Chickpea, Kale, and Lentil Stew on page 84.)

Great all year long: In the summer your kitchen stays cool while you prepare a meal with fresh ingredients, and in the winter you'll end up with a warm and comforting dish of plant-based food you know will be good for you. Strawberries and Cream Overnight Oatmeal (page 21) for breakfast is great when strawberries are fresh in the spring, and Comforting Tomato Soup (page 60) is delicious in the cooler months.

Hands-off cooking: A slow cooker is the ultimate multitasking tool. In many cases, you can set it and forget it and come back to a finished meal, like an amazingly satisfying Spinach Lasagna (page 116).

Deliciously developed flavors: Cooking low and slow allows flavors to develop and blend in delicious ways not usually achievable with other cooking methods. The Cauliflower, Chickpea, Quinoa, and Coconut Curry (page 77) benefits from the time it spends simmering.

Not Your Grandmother's Slow Cooker

Did you know that Irving Nachumsohn, the guy who invented an early version of the lava lamp, also invented the slow cooker? The appliance didn't become popular until the early 1970s after the Rival manufacturing company bought the patent rights and produced the first Crock-Pot, which became the name used for slow cookers for decades to follow. (In fact, when I first told my mom I was writing a slow cooker cookbook, she wasn't sure what I meant until I said, "It's a bunch of Crock-Pot recipes," to which she answered, "Oh, I didn't know it was called anything else!") Slow cookers have come a long way since the 1970s, but the basic cooking premise has remained the same: low and slow.

For the recipes in this book, all you'll need is a six-quart slow cooker with a High and a Low heat setting. There are many brands to choose from, but select a model that works best for your needs. Plan to set it and forget it while you're at work? Look for a slow cooker with an automatic timer and a "keep warm" feature, which come in handy when you've got a recipe that might take less time to cook than you want or when you want to throw in the ingredients and start the cooking process a while later. If you love the extra flavor imparted by sautéing ingredients before adding them to the slow cooker but want to skip an extra pan, look for a multipurpose model that has a sauté option. Then you can easily sauté and switch to slow cooking mode with the touch of a button.

TOOL TALK

While all you really need is a slow cooker, there are a few other tools that might make your time in the kitchen a bit easier. Here's my list of Felicia's Favorites.

HIGH-SPEED BLENDER: These can be pricey, but some come with extended guarantees and are well worth the investment. I use mine at least twice a day, every day. Look for models that run around 1,500 watts and 2 horsepower during blending to make quick work of creating 20-Minute Cashew Cheeze Sauce (page 141), for example, to incorporate into your slow cooker dishes.

IMMERSION BLENDER: When you've got a six-quart slow cooker full of near-boiling ingredients, an immersion blender, also known as a stick blender, is a safe and easy way to combine them. A model that works for your kitchen—cordless or corded—that is 200 to 250 watts is a good choice for blending creamy soups.

MINI FOOD PROCESSOR: If you have the first two items on the list, a full-size food processor isn't necessary. My immersion blender came with a mini food processor attachment, and I use it all the time for chopping nuts or onions when I'm in a hurry and need to get the ingredients into the slow cooker and run. It's easy to clean and fun to use.

SHARP CHEF'S KNIFE: Look for a knife that feels good in your hand, with the metal of the knife going up through the handle (called the "tang"). A good all-purpose chef's knife has an eight-inch blade and will make quick work of slicing and dicing ingredients. Plus, a sharp knife is always safer than a dull one.

SLOW COOKER LINERS, ALUMINUM FOIL, AND PARCHMENT: Look for "slow cooker liners" in the storage bag and aluminum foil section of your grocery store. I recommend using them for easy cleanup, especially for recipes that can be sticky like the Savory Slow Cooker Stuffing (page 49). You'll also note in some recipes, such as Chocolate's Best Friends Brownies (page 122), I use aluminum foil to create a collar on the inside of the slow cooker to keep the edges from cooking too quickly. Parchment is another tool in this category that will help keep food from sticking.

STORAGE SOLUTIONS: One of the wonders of slow cooking is making recipes to refrigerate or freeze for later. You can use glass Mason jars and plastic containers for storing leftovers in your refrigerator, as well as freezer-safe resealable bags and plastic containers for the foods that are freezable.

Slow Cooking Safely

Slow cookers are inherently easy to use, but a few safety tips will make sure you and your cooker stay in good working order.

- Always use your slow cooker on a flat, heat-safe surface, like your kitchen counter, away from any towels, papers, or clutter.

- If possible, use a slow cooker with a "keep warm" function so that after the cooking time, the pot will cool itself to stop cooking but not so much as to create an environment for harmful bacteria to grow (yuck!). If yours doesn't have this function, make sure you're home to remove the food to enjoy, refrigerate, or freeze.

- If using a second-hand slow cooker or using yours for the first time in a while, test it to be sure it heats properly. Fill it about three-fourths of the way with room-temperature water, set it to Low for eight hours, then use a food thermometer to measure the temperature of the water. You're looking for 185°F.

- To prepare food for cooking in advance, store your ingredients in a large covered container in the refrigerator and transfer everything to the slow cooker in the morning. Don't refrigerate the slow cooker's inner ceramic pot; the quick heat increase can cause it to crack.

- A few years ago, when I was in a hurry and wanted to sauté some ingredients before slow cooking, I put the ceramic pot of my cooker directly onto the gas burner. As the pot heated up, I suddenly heard a loud *crack!* While it didn't split in two, there was a hairline fracture up one side . . . so don't do that!

SLOW COOKER SAVVY

If you're new to cooking, or if you've had some mishaps that make you shy away from the kitchen, slow cooking is one of the best ways to find success. Whether you're a beginner or a culinary pro, the slow cooker can easily become your go-to appliance when you want a healthy meal with little prep. Follow these tips to get great results every time.

DON'T LIFT THE LID. While it may be tempting to check on your food as it cooks, unless the recipe calls for stirring the pot occasionally, keep the lid firmly in place and let the slow cooker work its magic. Each time you lift the lid, you lower the temperature in the pot, and your dish may require additional time to cook—up to 30 minutes.

DON'T OVERFILL YOUR SLOW COOKER. Overfilling your slow cooker makes the food steam rather than simmer. Both are wet cooking methods, but steaming isn't desirable for many recipes. Use a slow cooker that is large enough to make enough food for however many people you are feeding (most recipes in this book are suitable for four to six servings), and keep it no more than about two-thirds full.

DON'T UNDERFILL YOUR SLOW COOKER, EITHER. If your slow cooker isn't about halfway full, your food is likely to burn before the end of the cooking time.

FILL THE SLOW COOKER IN THE ORDER THE RECIPE STATES. Yes, with some recipes and ingredients you can "dump and go," but others require a specific order. Keep in mind, the hottest part of the slow cooker is at the bottom, so as you begin to experiment with your own recipes, first add ingredients that take longer to cook, such as root vegetables chopped into larger pieces, and finish with more finely chopped foods.

DON'T OVERCOOK. Especially with plant-based recipes, pay attention to the cooking time or else you could end up with a bowl of unappealing mush or a dish burned beyond salvaging. Use the appropriate heat level and cooking time to ensure your meals are picture-perfect and taste as good as they look.

PLANT-BASED SLOW COOKING

As I mentioned, when I first transitioned to a primarily plant-based diet, I quit using my slow cooker. With all the veggies and quick-cooking grains, most of the recipes I found could be easily prepared in less than an hour, and I didn't understand why you'd want it to take longer. Then I started seeing friends make plant-based foods in their slow cookers, and I was reminded how convenient it is to put in my ingredients and go about my day. In this section, we'll talk about how slow cooking and plant-based foods can work together for easy, delicious results.

How Slow Can We Go?

While one of the benefits of slow cooking is a long hands-off cooking time, the truth is that most plant-based recipes beyond dried beans don't need eight hours to develop flavors or fully cook the ingredients. So how slow *can* we go with plant-based ingredients? It depends.

In some recipes, you'll see more tender veggies like zucchini added later in the cooking process to maintain their texture, like in the Minestrone Soup (page 71). For other recipes, like the Three Bean and Barley White Chili (page 89), you can put everything in and walk away from the slow cooker until it's time to eat.

Each of the recipes in this book was either created for the slow cooker or adapted from stovetop or oven recipes, with times and ingredients adjusted for optimum slow cooking results. Some can be cooked for longer periods of time on Low (see the following list), while others don't need much more than a couple of hours. When cooking on High for a shorter time is an option, both times are listed.

Also, keep in mind that every slow cooker is different. Throughout this book, you'll see as much as a two-hour range for some of the cooking times (six to eight hours, for example). You'll have to experiment with your particular slow cooker to determine the best cooking times for your favorite recipes.

If you're looking for hands-off recipes that take a bit longer to make, here are a few to try.

- For a hearty breakfast waiting for you after cooking overnight—a full seven to eight hours on Low—try the Maple, Apple, and Walnut Great Grains (page 20).

- Rosemary-Onion Jam (page 30) is a delicious appetizer that can take up to 12 hours on Low for the onions to caramelize.

- The broth in Shiitake, Lemongrass, and Rice Noodle Pho (page 78) takes a good long time to properly develop the flavors. You add the noodles at the end and top it with fresh basil, cilantro, bean sprouts, and scallions.

- Any of the blended soups work well because you can't overcook the ingredients. I love the rich Golden Split Pea Soup (page 67), the sweet Butternut Squash Soup (page 70), or my plant-based version of the French classic Potato-Leek Soup (page 62), all of which can take up to eight hours on Low to cook.

- Many of the dinners in this book can cook for up to eight hours on Low, including the spicy Cajun-Style Jambalaya (page 114).

- If you need a slow-cooking dessert, try the Pumpkin Pie Oatmeal Parfaits (page 121), which take seven hours on Low and have a beautiful presentation.

A Plant-Based Pantry

It doesn't take a lot of fancy ingredients to have a pantry stocked for plant-based slow cooking. Here are the basics you'll see used throughout this book, as well as some information on how to best make them work for the slow cooker and your diet.

Beans and legumes: Beans and legumes are an excellent source of protein. Most of my recipes call for canned beans because they are easy to find and to use. Depending on the bean, one can of beans is about 1½ cups, so if you cook dried beans, store them in the freezer in 1- to 2-cup portions. I use canned lentils occasionally, but in recipes such as the Lentil Sloppy Joes (page 110), dried lentils cook up perfectly.

Canned goods: Look for no-salt-added and no-sugar-added varieties whenever possible. Even some large store brands offer no-salt and no-sugar options. In those recipes where a canned ingredient is preferred, I call for it and note whether you can substitute with fresh.

Condiments: You'd be surprised by some ingredient labels. For example, since Worcestershire sauce is typically made with anchovies, you'll find a delicious and easy-to-make plant-based version on page 139, or you can search out plant-based brands online. Soy sauce is used to flavor many recipes, but if you're watching your sodium intake, look for low-sodium varieties or use a lower-sodium tamari sauce. Coconut aminos have a similar flavor profile without the sodium.

Egg alternatives: Depending on its purpose in a recipe, you'll have multiple options. Aquafaba is the liquid inside a can of chickpeas, and it works well in baked goods like my Lemon Poppy Seed Cake (page 130). Flax eggs are 1 tablespoon of ground flaxseed (also called flaxseed meal) mixed with 2½ tablespoons of water. I use them in recipes like Poppy's Carrot Cake (page 126) for a more combined texture. Sometimes a recipe calls for tofu to replace eggs, such as in the Southwestern-Style Breakfast Burritos (page 26), where the tofu is crumbled and mixed with a tiny bit of turmeric for color and added nutrition.

Fresh and frozen vegetables: Most of the time, you can easily substitute a frozen vegetable for fresh, especially if you want to cut down on prep work. You can find chopped onions in the frozen food aisle at the grocery store and use them in almost every recipe in chapter 5. One medium onion is about 2 cups of chopped frozen onions. Other frozen veggies that are easy swaps for fresh are bell peppers, corn, carrots, and green beans. You could also buy fresh veggies and do the prep work yourself, freezing chopped onions, peppers, celery, and carrots in 1- to 2-cup portions. Place them in resealable freezer bags and use them as you would fresh in these recipes.

Meat and dairy alternatives: As with anything packaged, I encourage you to carefully read the labels to determine if a product's ingredients suit your dietary needs. For example, most dairy and meat alternatives are processed, high in oil and salt, and unable to fit into a WFPBSOS diet. However, if you're trying to eat plant-based in a broader sense, you may find the transition easier if you have some familiar items like faux meats and dairy alternatives. You'll see suggestions for how to use them in many of these recipes.

Oil alternatives: If you are trying to lose weight eating a plant-based diet, I have good news for you: you don't need to cook with oil to get loads of flavor. None of these recipes use oil, and I don't think you'll miss it. All plant-based foods have their own amount of water and/or oil stored inside the plant cells themselves. In baked goods like Gooey Bittersweet Chocolate Pudding Cake (page 124), you can use applesauce for moistness. For sautéing, I sometimes use a splash of veggie broth or even water, but I often start with a hot, dry pan and find the liquid released by the cooking veggies is sufficient.

Plant-based milks: You can find milks made from soy, almonds, cashews, coconuts, rice, hemp, oats, and more in most grocery stores. When these recipes call for "unsweetened plant-based milk," choose your favorite plain variety. Occasionally I call for a specific milk, such as full-fat canned coconut milk in the Thai-Inspired Coconut Cabbage Soup (page 68), and in that case the recipe will be best with that type of milk.

Vegetable broth: It's so easy to make your own veggie broth, and it's a great way to control the amount of sodium and additives. You'll find a recipe for Low-Sodium Vegetable Broth on page 136, and I hope you'll consider the eco-friendly way I suggest making it in the headnote (which will be a snap with these recipes).

Plant-Based Slow Cooking Like a Pro

There are a few things to keep in mind when you're using plant-based ingredients in your slow cooker. Here are some tips to get the most delicious results.

Save fresh herbs for last. I have an herb garden and love tossing fresh herbs into my dishes; however, most fresh herbs are too delicate to be slow cooked. Some recipes use hardier herbs, like a fresh bay leaf or a sprig of woody rosemary, in the beginning of cooking and then call for you to pluck them out before serving. A simple rule is to use dried herbs for cooking and add fresh herbs in the last 30 minutes or as a garnish.

Cut ingredients uniformly. You don't have to be as precise as a Michelin-starred chef when you dice your onions or cut your potatoes, but you definitely want to make sure all like ingredients are roughly the same size so you don't end up with some smaller pieces turned to mush while larger hunks aren't cooked through. I've included the sizes to cut each ingredient for optimum cooking in that recipe.

Avoid the acid. I have a short story for you: When I was testing the British Beans on Toast (page 24), I started with dried navy beans. Even after 48 *hours* of slow cooking—two full days—they *never* became soft enough to fully enjoy. Why? Because I was cooking them with a can of tomatoes, and the acid prevented the beans from cooking properly. Don't make my mistake. Acid and beans don't get along until after the beans are softened.

A NOTE ABOUT CHOOSING ORGANIC FOODS

As I mentioned before, there are so many benefits to choosing a plant-based lifestyle, and I agree with Dr. Michael Greger, founder of NutritionFacts.org, when he says, "We should never let concern about pesticides stop us from stuffing our face with as many fruits and vegetables as possible." However, if it's within your budget and ability, I suggest opting for certified organic ingredients when you can. You will be not only avoiding harmful pesticides and genetically modified organisms (GMOs), but also supporting the health of farm workers and the insect pollinator friends that do the heavy lifting to make crops grow.

I know that a grocery bill can really add up, so if you don't have it in your budget to go full-on organic, each year the Environmental Working Group publishes a list of which fruits and vegetables are better purchased as organic (Dirty Dozen™) and which are safe to eat conventionally (Clean 15™). The 2020 lists include the following.

Dirty Dozen™

- Apples
- Celery
- Cherries
- Grapes
- Kale
- Nectarines
- Peaches
- Pears
- Potatoes
- Spinach
- Strawberries
- Tomatoes

Clean 15™

- Asparagus
- Avocado
- Broccoli
- Cabbage
- Cantaloupe
- Cauliflower
- Eggplant
- Honey dew melon
- Kiwi
- Mushrooms
- Onions
- Papaya
- Pineapple
- Sweet corn
- Sweet peas, frozen

Line your cooker. Some ingredients, like oats and rice, will stick to the slow cooker. That's why it's important to prep the slow cooker with a liner, parchment paper, or cooking spray. In the case of some desserts, you can make a sort-of sling with handles to pull the baked goods out of the slow cooker after cooking. (See page 5 for more information on liners.)

Keep condensation away. Although the moist environment of the slow cooker is ideal for many foods, some dishes such as Nutty Granola with Power Seeds and Dried Fruit (page 18) or Peach Cobbler (page 123) can become soggy unless you use a simple trick. To keep the condensation that forms on the inside of the lid away from the food as it cooks, stretch a clean dish towel or several layers of paper towels across the top of the slow cooker—not touching the food—and place the lid on top of the towel(s). In some cases, like the Crispy Chickpea Snackers (page 39), you'll even prop the lid open to allow steam to escape.

Thicken the plant-based way. Whenever possible, I try to use a whole food to thicken my sauces. For example, in the Creamy Corn Chowder (page 81), I blend the soup itself to make it thick and creamy. In the Mushroom Stroganoff (page 104), I blend cashews and nutritional yeast with plant-based milk to give it that touch of smoothness and thickness at the end of cooking.

LET'S GET (SLOW) COOKING!

On the following pages you'll find one hundred plant-based recipes developed specifically for the slow cooker. Whether you're just getting started with plant-based cooking or you're looking for more convenience in your plant-based lifestyle, you'll find something to meet your needs. And whatever version of plant-based lifestyle you lead, you'll be able to make these dishes work for you. They're all free of oil and refined sugar, and where salt is listed, it is an optional ingredient you can add to taste or not at all.

While most of the recipes are stand-alone dishes, you'll find a chapter of SOS-free basics and bonus recipes that, aside from my delicious Mama Mia Marinara Sauce (page 150), don't require the slow cooker. These can be used to add flavor, texture, and a little pizazz, like the Shredded Tofu Meaty Crumbles (page 146), the Greener Guacamole (page 145), or my Plant-Based Fish Sauce (page 138).

But where to start? Let's say you're craving a hearty, stick-to-your-ribs breakfast. I suggest the Sweet Potato and Black Bean Hash (page 25). For a feel-good lunch that might take you back to your childhood, make up a batch of the Comforting Tomato Soup (page 60)—and instead of croutons, whip up a batch of the Crispy Chickpea

Snackers (page 39) to drop on top. (You may never want boring old oyster crackers again!) When you need a quick and easy dinner, try a Southern favorite: Black-Eyed Peas and Collard Greens with Brown Rice (page 95), a classic dish served with some peppery vinegar. Time for dessert? The slow cooker can handle that, too. Creamy Dreamy Brown Rice Pudding (page 120) will warm your heart, as well as your belly.

Recipe Labels and Tips

So you can easily find the recipe that works best for your needs and get the most out of every dish, each recipe has labels and tips. There are labels for dietary needs or preferences like Gluten-free, Soy-free, and Nut-free. And if a dish can be frozen, you'll see the Freezable label. Here are the tips you can find.

Cooking Tip: These are suggestions for preparing the food, hacks to cut down prep time, and other details worth keeping in mind while cooking.

Ingredient Tip: You'll find information on where to purchase or how best to use ingredients.

Leftovers Tip: These explain how best to store and reheat the dish.

Variation Tip: These will put a new twist on the recipe by adding ingredients or suggesting substitutions to spark your creativity and imagination.

> **A NOTE ON ALLERGENS:** When dealing with allergens, be sure to read your labels carefully and use your best judgment. For example, if you are looking for a gluten-free product, such as oats, make sure it has the certified gluten-free label. People with tree nut allergies often wonder if they should avoid coconut. My understanding is that even though the US Food and Drug Administration (FDA) recognizes it as a tree nut, it is a fruit. While allergic reactions have been documented, most people with tree nut allergies can safely eat coconut. If you are allergic to tree nuts, talk to your allergist before adding coconut to your diet.

CHAPTER TWO

Breakfasts

Nutty Granola with Power Seeds
and Dried Fruit
18

Maple, Apple, and
Walnut Great Grains
20

Strawberries and
Cream Overnight Oatmeal
21

Blueberry, Cinnamon, and
Pecan French Toast
22

Potato and Veggie
Breakfast Casserole
23

British Beans
on Toast
24

Sweet Potato and
Black Bean Hash
25

Southwestern-Style
Breakfast Burritos
26

Gluten-free, Soy-free

Nutty Granola with Power Seeds and Dried Fruit

MAKES: 10 cups | **PREP TIME:** 15 minutes | **COOK TIME:** 6 hours on Low, plus 45 to 60 minutes to cool

Ever since he was a kid, every night before bed my husband has eaten a bowl of cereal. Whenever I make this granola, it's his go-to nighttime nosh, and I feel better knowing exactly what's in his bowl. I eat this hearty, nutty granola for breakfast many mornings with a bit of unsweetened vanilla almond or soy milk.

1 overripe
   banana, peeled

3 tablespoons water

6 cups old-
   fashioned oats

½ cup chopped pecans

½ cup chopped walnuts

½ cup raw cashews

½ cup slivered or
   chopped raw almonds

½ cup unsweetened
   coconut flakes

3 tablespoons ground
   flaxseed

3 tablespoons
   raw pepitas

3 tablespoons raw
   sunflower seeds

3 tablespoons
   chia seeds

½ cup maple syrup

½ cup aquafaba (see
   page 10)

½ cup raisins

½ cup currants

½ cup unsweetened
   dried cherries

1. In the bottom of the slow cooker, mash together the banana and water. Add the oats, pecans, walnuts, cashews, almonds, coconut, flaxseed, pepitas, sunflower seeds, chia seeds, and maple syrup.

2. In a small bowl, use an electric beater to whip the aquafaba into almost-stiff peaks, about 5 minutes. Add it to the slow cooker and stir to combine.

3. To keep the condensation that forms on the inside of the lid away from the granola, stretch a clean dish towel or several layers of paper towels over the top of the slow cooker, but not touching the food, and place the lid on top of the towel(s). Cook on Low for 6 hours, stirring every hour to make sure the granola does not burn and replacing the damp towels as needed.

4. After 6 hours, the granola will be darker in color. Transfer it to a parchment-lined baking sheet, spread it out, and let it cool for up to 1 hour. Once it's completely cool and crispy, sprinkle on the raisins, currants, and dried cherries and stir to combine. Store in a large airtight container for up to 2 weeks.

Per serving (½ cup): Calories: 265; Fat: 12g; Carbohydrates: 36g; Protein: 7g; Fiber: 6g; Sodium: 5mg

VARIATION TIP: You can vary this as much as you'd like, maintaining the ratios. Add different unsweetened dried fruits, such as cranberries, blueberries, or apricot pieces, or try different nuts, such as raw hazelnuts or pistachios.

Soy-free

Maple, Apple, and Walnut Great Grains

SERVES: 4 to 6 | **PREP TIME:** 10 minutes | **COOK TIME:** 3 to 4 hours on High or 7 to 8 hours on Low

Including a variety of whole grains in your diet is as good for your soul as it is for your gut health. A warm, hearty bowl of this fiber-filled breakfast will keep you satisfied all morning. Choose sweeter varieties of apples like Gala or Fuji. If you don't have all the various grains handy, you can swap them out for each other fairly easily, but do try to use the mixture as written because the result in texture is extraordinary.

2 large apples

½ cup quinoa, rinsed

½ cup steel-cut oats

½ cup wheatberries

½ cup pearl barley

½ cup bulgur wheat

1 tablespoon ground flaxseed

2 teaspoons ground cinnamon

½ teaspoon ground or grated nutmeg

7 cups water

⅓ cup maple syrup

½ cup chopped walnuts

½ cup raisins

Unsweetened plant-based milk, for serving (optional)

1. Peel, core, and chop the apples and place them in the slow cooker. Add the quinoa, oats, wheatberries, barley, bulgur wheat, flaxseed, cinnamon, nutmeg, water, and maple syrup. Stir gently. Cover and cook on High for 3 to 4 hours or on Low for 7 to 8 hours.

2. Before serving, stir in the walnuts and raisins. Spoon into a bowl and add your favorite milk (if using).

Per serving: Calories: 691; Fat: 13g; Carbohydrates: 133g; Protein: 18g; Fiber: 21g; Sodium: 16mg

INGREDIENT TIP: Wheatberries are a readily available grain with a texture that's a cross between rice and bulgur wheat or farro. They may be found in the rice and beans section of your grocery store, in the baking aisle with similar grains, or in the international aisle.

VARIATION TIP: Swap out the raisins for other dried fruit, such as currants or chopped dates. For even more protein and fiber, stir in some pumpkin seeds and experiment with your favorite nuts, like pecans or almonds.

Gluten-free, Nut-free, Soy-free

Strawberries and Cream Overnight Oatmeal

SERVES: 4 to 6 | **PREP TIME:** 5 minutes | **COOK TIME:** 4 to 5 hours on High or 8 to 9 hours on Low

Oh my yum. Cooking steel-cut oats overnight in the slow cooker is an awesome way to enjoy them for breakfast in the morning without the wait of conventional stove cooking. This recipe uses a bit of plant-based milk to cook the oats, which provides the creamy flavor and consistency. Sprinkling ground flaxseed after cooking adds another layer of texture, and the fresh strawberries brighten up the whole bowl.

Nonstick cooking spray (optional)

1¼ cups steel-cut oats

4 cups water

1⅔ cups unsweetened plant-based milk

2 teaspoons vanilla extract

¼ cup maple syrup

3 tablespoons ground flaxseed

1 pound fresh strawberries, stemmed and sliced

1. Coat the inside of the slow cooker with cooking spray (if using) or line it with a slow cooker liner.

2. Place the oats, water, milk, vanilla, and maple syrup in the slow cooker. Cover and cook on High for 4 to 5 hours or on Low for 8 to 9 hours.

3. When ready to serve, stir the flaxseed into the oatmeal and portion into bowls. Top each with 3 to 5 sliced strawberries.

Per serving: Calories: 320; Fat: 7g; Carbohydrates: 59g; Protein: 9g; Fiber: 9g; Sodium: 64mg

INGREDIENT TIP: Using old-fashioned oats leads to a gloppy mess. And don't even think about trying instant oats. Steel-cut oats are denser and take longer to cook, so they are perfect for the slow cooker. It might not seem like enough ingredients, but the oats grow in size as they absorb the liquid and become toothsome and delicious.

VARIATION TIP: Make this blueberries and cream or peaches and cream or raspberries and cream—you get it—by adding your favorite fruit instead of (or in addition to!) the strawberries. Topping the dish with nuts can give crunch and texture.

Soy-free

Blueberry, Cinnamon, and Pecan French Toast

SERVES: 4 to 6 | **PREP TIME:** 10 minutes, plus 30 to 60 minutes soaking time
COOK TIME: 2 to 3 hours on High or 4 to 5 hours on Low

When I was a little girl, French toast was my favorite Sunday morning breakfast. This casserole version brings back the flavors I remember—the warmth of the cinnamon and vanilla custard—updated to be plant-based and every bit as delicious.

2 tablespoons ground flaxseed

5 tablespoons water

1 (16-ounce) loaf crusty whole-grain bread

1 overripe banana, peeled

1 (14.5-ounce) can full-fat coconut milk

1 cup unsweetened plant-based milk

1 tablespoon chia seeds

1 teaspoon ground cinnamon

1 tablespoon vanilla extract

Nonstick cooking spray (optional)

2 cups fresh or frozen blueberries, divided

¼ cup chopped pecans, for serving

Maple syrup, for serving

1. In a small bowl or ramekin, stir together the flaxseed and water to form flax eggs. Let rest while preparing the remaining ingredients.

2. Slice the bread into 1- to 2-inch chunks and place in a large casserole dish deep enough to have the bread submerged in the custard.

3. Place the banana, coconut milk, plant-based milk, chia seeds, cinnamon, vanilla, and flax eggs in a blender. Blend to combine and pour over the bread. Cover and refrigerate for at least 30 minutes to allow the bread to soak up the custard.

4. Coat the inside of the slow cooker with cooking spray (if using) or line it with a slow cooker liner. Remove the bread and custard mixture from refrigerator and place half in the bottom of the slow cooker. Add 1 cup of blueberries, then layer the remaining half of the bread and custard mixture. Top with the remaining 1 cup of blueberries. Cover and cook on High for 2 to 3 hours or on Low for 4 to 5 hours.

5. To serve, top each portion with a tablespoon of pecans and a drizzle of maple syrup.

Per serving: Calories: 644; Fat: 31g; Carbohydrates: 81g; Protein: 5g; Fiber: 18g; Sodium: 336g

Gluten-free, Nut-free

Potato and Veggie Breakfast Casserole

SERVES: 4 to 6 | **PREP TIME:** 10 minutes | **COOK TIME:** 4 to 5 hours on High or 7 to 8 hours on Low

When I first began eating plant-based food, I wasn't so sure about tofu replacing eggs, but the texture is similar and the tofu takes on the flavors of the seasonings and the veggies. Plus, the turmeric in this dish will make the tofu the color of scrambled eggs. In my house, I always serve savory breakfast dishes with a dash of our favorite hot sauce.

1 medium red bell pepper, diced

1 medium onion, diced

1 (8-ounce) package white button or cremini mushrooms, quartered

3 cups chopped kale

Ground black pepper

Salt (optional)

1 teaspoon garlic powder, divided

1 teaspoon onion powder, divided

1 teaspoon paprika, divided

1 (14-ounce) package extra-firm tofu, drained

1 teaspoon ground turmeric

8 small Yukon Gold or red potatoes (about 2 pounds), unpeeled and sliced into half-inch rounds

1. Place the bell pepper, onion, mushrooms, and kale in the slow cooker. Season with pepper and salt (if using). Add ½ teaspoon each of the garlic powder, onion powder, and paprika. Mix to distribute the seasonings.

2. Crumble the tofu directly into the slow cooker. Sprinkle the tofu with the turmeric and stir until the tofu is coated. Then mix the tofu and veggies together.

3. Layer the potatoes on top of the veggies and tofu. Sprinkle with the remaining ½ teaspoon each of garlic powder, onion powder, and paprika. Season again with salt (if using) and pepper. Cover and cook on High for 4 to 5 hours or on Low for 7 to 8 hours.

Per serving: Calories: 334; Fat: 6g; Carbohydrates: 54g; Protein: 18g; Fiber: 7g; Sodium: 36mg

VARIATION TIP: Cook crumbled or sliced plant-based sausage according to the package directions. Add it with the onions into the slow cooker. Top with shredded dairy-free cheeze in the last 15 minutes of cook time, if desired.

Nut-free, Freezable

British Beans on Toast

SERVES: 6 | **PREP TIME:** 10 minutes | **COOK TIME:** 3 to 4 hours on High or 7 to 8 hours on Low

British baked beans are different from the perhaps more familiar Boston baked beans or BBQ baked beans common in US kitchens. British-style beans have a slightly less sweet flavor with a tomato tang. They have long been a favorite part of a traditional English breakfast and are usually served on toast. Maybe they'll become a new favorite for you, too!

3 (14.5-ounce) cans navy beans, drained and rinsed

1 medium onion, coarsely chopped

4 garlic cloves, minced

1 (14-ounce) can no-salt-added crushed tomatoes

¾ cup Low-Sodium Vegetable Broth (page 136) or store-bought

½ cup unsweetened apple juice

¼ cup maple syrup

3 tablespoons apple cider vinegar

1 tablespoon Plant-Based Worcestershire Sauce (page 139) or store-bought

2 bay leaves

½ teaspoon paprika

½ teaspoon ground black pepper

Salt (optional)

6 slices whole-wheat bread, toasted

1. Place the beans, onion, garlic, tomatoes, broth, apple juice, maple syrup, vinegar, Worcestershire sauce, bay leaves, paprika, and pepper in the slow cooker. Mix well and cook on High for 3 to 4 hours or on Low for 7 to 8 hours. If adding salt, wait until after the cooking time has ended as salt can make the beans tough.

2. Remove and discard the bay leaves. Spoon about ¼ cup of beans over each slice of toast to serve. The beans will keep refrigerated in a container for 3 to 4 days or frozen for 2 to 3 months.

Per serving: Calories: 334; Fat: 2g; Carbohydrates: 65g; Protein: 15g; Fiber: 15g; Sodium: 273g

COOKING TIP: If you're cooking for a crowd, toast your bread on a baking sheet in the oven under the broiler to have all the pieces done at the same time. Just don't walk away from it because toast can burn quickly.

Gluten-free, Nut-free, Soy-free

Sweet Potato and Black Bean Hash

SERVES: 4 to 6 | **PREP TIME:** 10 minutes | **COOK TIME:** 2 to 3 hours on Low

I didn't try breakfast hash until my adult years, and since that first taste I could never get enough. This recipe includes black beans for added protein, and the shallot gives the dish a nice mellow flavor that lets the sweetness of the sweet potatoes shine through. Adding the plant-based milk at the end gives this hash a luscious creamy sauce that coats the whole dish.

1 shallot, diced

2 cups peeled, chopped sweet potatoes (about 1 large or 2 small)

1 medium bell pepper (any color), diced

2 garlic cloves, minced

1 (14.5-ounce) can black beans, drained and rinsed

1 teaspoon paprika

½ teaspoon onion powder

½ teaspoon garlic powder

¼ cup Low-Sodium Vegetable Broth (page 136) or store-bought

4 to 6 tablespoons unsweetened plant-based milk

1. Place the shallot, sweet potatoes, bell pepper, garlic, beans, paprika, onion powder, garlic powder, and broth in the slow cooker. Stir to combine. Cover and cook on Low for 2 to 3 hours, until the potatoes are soft.

2. Remove the lid and add the milk, starting with 4 tablespoons, and stir to combine. You're looking for a creamy sauce to develop. Add more milk as needed and allow to heat through for a few minutes before serving.

Per serving: Calories: 251; Fat: 1g; Carbohydrates: 53g; Protein: 9g; Fiber: 14g; Sodium: 90mg

Nut-Free, Freezable

Southwestern-Style Breakfast Burritos

SERVES: 4 to 6 | **PREP TIME:** 10 minutes | **COOK TIME:** 2 to 3 hours on High or 5 to 6 hours on Low

For south-of-the-border flair—or a healthy one-hand breakfast on the go—these burritos hit the spot. I add a dollop of my Greener Guacamole (page 145) before rolling and eating. To speed up prep time, replace the onions, garlic, bell pepper, and canned tomatoes with a large jar of your favorite salsa.

1 medium onion, diced

1 medium red bell pepper, diced

3 garlic cloves, minced

1 (10-ounce) package frozen corn

1 (14-ounce) can pinto beans, drained and rinsed

1 (14-ounce) can no-salt-added diced tomatoes

2 handfuls chopped kale (about 2 heaping cups)

1 (14-ounce) package extra-firm tofu

1 teaspoon ground turmeric

1 tablespoon chili powder

3 tablespoons nutritional yeast

Salt (optional)

Ground black pepper

6 to 8 (10-inch) whole-grain tortillas

1. Place the onion, bell pepper, and garlic in the slow cooker. Add the corn, beans, tomatoes, and kale. Crumble the tofu over the vegetables to look like scrambled eggs. Sprinkle the turmeric over the tofu and stir to coat, until the tofu is the color of scrambled eggs. Add the chili powder, nutritional yeast, salt (if using), and black pepper. Stir to combine. Cover and cook on High for 2 to 3 hours or on Low for 5 to 6 hours.

2. Using a slotted spoon to drain off excess liquid, scoop about ⅓ cup of burrito filling onto the center of each tortilla. Roll the bottom of the tortilla to cover the filling, fold one side over the filling, and continue rolling to close.

Per serving: Calories: 632; Fat: 15g; Carbohydrates: 98g; Protein: 32g; Fiber: 18g; Sodium: 1,010mg

LEFTOVERS TIP: Wrap the burritos in wax paper and store in a resealable freezer bag or freeze the filling separately. From frozen, reheat in the microwave for 2 to 3 minutes, until warmed through.

VARIATION TIP: Add plant-based chorizo at the beginning of the cooking time or top your burritos with plant-based cheeze and/or sour cream.

CHAPTER THREE

Snacks and Appetizers

Rosemary-Onion Jam
30

Pineapple, Peach, and
Mango Salsa
31

Spinach-Artichoke Dip
32

White Bean Tzatziki Dip
34

Buffalo Cauliflower Dip
35

Creamy Southwestern
Salsa Bean Dip
36

Eggplant Caponata Bruschetta
37

Sweet 'n' Spicy Crunchy
Snack Mix
38

Crispy Chickpea Snackers
39

Spiced Glazed Carrots
40

Classic Italian Mushrooms
41

Cheezy Stuffed Potato Skins
42

< White Bean
Tzatziki Dip,
Page 34

Gluten-free, Nut-free, Soy-free

Rosemary-Onion Jam

MAKES: 3 to 4 cups | **PREP TIME:** 5 minutes | **COOK TIME:** 6 to 7 hours on High or 10 to 12 hours on Low

The slow cooker is like magic, bringing foods that need to cook low and slow to life in a whole different way. Usually, the humble onion acts as a flavor base allowing other ingredients to shine, but the long cook time here allows the onions to caramelize and become the star of the show. This jam is a little bit sweet, a little bit tangy, and just perfect for slathering on crostini for an appetizer, as a topping for baked potatoes, or even as a relish or condiment for sandwiches or veggie burgers. It's delicious served warm or cold.

4 to 6 large sweet onions (about 3 pounds), sliced into half-moons

2 garlic cloves, minced

½ cup maple syrup

¼ cup balsamic vinegar

1 teaspoon finely chopped fresh rosemary (about 2 sprigs), or dried

1. Put the onions in the slow cooker. Add the garlic.

2. In a small bowl, stir together the maple syrup, vinegar, and rosemary. Pour the mixture into the slow cooker and toss gently to coat the onions. Cover and cook on High for 6 to 7 hours or on Low for 10 to 12 hours, until the onions are deep brown.

3. Transfer the mixture to a blender, or use an immersion blender, and blend into a chunky jam consistency. Store in glass jars or plastic containers in the refrigerator for up to 1 month.

Per serving (¼ cup): Calories: 76; Fat: <1g; Carbohydrates: 19g; Protein: 1g; Fiber: 1g; Sodium: 12mg

Gluten-free, Nut-free, Soy-free

Pineapple, Peach, and Mango Salsa

MAKES: about 6 cups | **PREP TIME:** 15 minutes | **COOK TIME:** 2 to 3 hours on Low

Depending on where you live, certain fresh fruits are only readily available in the summer months, but you can find canned fruits all year long—and with this bright, fruity salsa, you'll enjoy a taste of summer anytime. Be sure to look for the canned fruit packed in 100 percent fruit juice, not syrup, to avoid added sugars.

1 medium onion, finely diced

2 garlic cloves, minced

1 medium orange, red, or yellow bell pepper, finely diced

1 (20-ounce) can crushed pineapple in juice

1 (15-ounce) can no-sugar-added mango in juice, drained and finely diced

1 (15-ounce) can no-sugar-added sliced peaches in juice, drained and finely diced

½ teaspoon ground cumin

1 teaspoon paprika

Juice of 1 lime

3 to 4 tablespoons chopped fresh mint (about 10 to 15 leaves)

1. Put the onion, garlic, and bell pepper in the slow cooker. Add the pineapple and its juices, the mango, and the peaches. Sprinkle the cumin and paprika into the slow cooker. Add the lime juice and stir well to combine.

2. Cover and cook on Low for 2 to 3 hours, or until the onion and peppers are cooked through and softened. Let the salsa cool slightly, then stir in the mint just before serving.

Per serving (¼ cup): Calories: 36; Fat: <1g; Carbohydrates: 9g; Protein: 1g; Fiber: 1g; Sodium: 2mg

VARIATION TIP: For a spicy Southwestern flair, replace the mint with cilantro and incorporate one finely diced jalapeño pepper, ½ teaspoon of chili powder, and an extra clove of minced garlic (optional) at the beginning of the cooking time. Stir in the cilantro after slightly cooling the finished dish.

Spinach-Artichoke Dip

MAKES: about 5 cups | **PREP TIME:** 20 minutes | **COOK TIME:** 2 hours on Low

Spinach-artichoke dip is a classic appetizer and has long been a favorite of mine. I've always served it in a bread bowl, with large pieces of bread cut from the hollowed-out center for dipping. Crackers or crudités are also delicious pairings. Crunchy water chestnuts give texture to this typically creamy dip. You won't want to wait for company to make this dish.

1 cup water

¾ cup raw cashews

1 (8-ounce) can water chestnuts, drained

1 (12-ounce) package frozen quartered or chopped artichoke hearts

1 (12-ounce) package frozen spinach

¼ cup finely chopped onion

2 garlic cloves, minced

1½ cups unsweetened plant-based milk

3 tablespoons nutritional yeast

1 tablespoon Plant-Based Worcestershire Sauce (page 139) or store-bought

1 tablespoon white miso paste

1 tablespoon lemon juice

½ teaspoon paprika

1. Boil the water and put the cashews in a medium bowl. Pour the hot water over the cashews and let soak to soften while you prepare the rest of the ingredients, at least 15 minutes.

2. Meanwhile, coarsely chop the water chestnuts and any artichoke hearts that are larger than bite-size. Add the water chestnuts, artichoke hearts, spinach, and onion to the slow cooker.

3. Drain the cashews. Put the cashews, garlic, milk, nutritional yeast, Worcestershire sauce, miso paste, lemon juice, and paprika in a blender. Blend on high until the sauce is very smooth and creamy.

4. Pour the sauce into the slow cooker and stir well to combine. The sauce will look a bit too thin at this stage, but it will thicken as the dip cooks. Cover and cook on Low for 2 hours, or until heated through. Store leftovers in the refrigerator for up to 4 days and reheat in the microwave until warmed through.

Per serving (¼ cup): Calories: 53; Fat: 3g; Carbohydrates: 6g; Protein: 3g; Fiber: 2g; Sodium: 81mg

VARIATION TIP: Turn these into stuffed jalapeño poppers. Slice off the stems and remove the seeds from jalapeño peppers. Stuff them with the dip and place them on a rimmed baking sheet. Place under the broiler for 6 to 7 minutes, until slightly charred, turning them over halfway through the cooking time.

Gluten-free, Nut-free, Soy-free

White Bean Tzatziki Dip

MAKES: about 8 cups | **PREP TIME:** 10 minutes | **COOK TIME:** 1 to 2 hours on Low

The bright flavors of Greece come to life in this bean dip that is reminiscent of a creamy tzatziki sauce, which traditionally uses Greek yogurt. Rather than try to replace the yogurt with a plant-based version, you'll get the same creaminess from the beans (cannellini or Great Northern work great here) and the crunch from the cooling lemon, dill, and cucumber topping. You can serve it with whole-wheat pitas or your favorite dippable veggies, but it's so good that you might want to eat it with a spoon!

4 (14.5-ounce) cans white beans, drained and rinsed

8 garlic cloves, minced

1 medium onion, coarsely chopped

¼ cup Low-Sodium Vegetable Broth (page 136) or store-bought, plus more as needed

Juice from one lemon, divided

2 teaspoons dried dill, divided

Salt (optional)

1 cucumber, peeled and finely diced

1. Place the beans, garlic, onion, broth, and half the lemon juice in a blender. Blend until creamy, about 1 minute, adding up to ¼ cup of additional broth as needed to make the mixture creamy.

2. Transfer the mixture to the slow cooker, stir in 1 teaspoon of dill, and season with salt (if using). Cover and cook on Low for 1 to 2 hours until heated through.

3. Meanwhile, in a medium bowl, mix the cucumber with the remaining 1 teaspoon of dill and the remaining half of the lemon juice. Toss to coat. Season with salt (if using).

4. Spoon the dip from the slow cooker into a serving bowl and top with the cucumber mixture before serving.

Per serving (¼ cup): Calories: 59; Fat: <1g; Carbohydrates: 11g; Protein: 3g; Fiber: 4g; Sodium: 1mg

Gluten-free

Buffalo Cauliflower Dip

MAKES: about 5 cups | **PREP TIME:** 20 minutes | **COOK TIME:** 2 hours on Low

For some people it's not game day without a serving of that spicy Buffalo taste, and this dip definitely hits the spot! Most hot pepper sauces are loaded with salt, but this recipe creates all the familiar flavors using a vinegar and cayenne mixture that gives a kick without any added sodium. I've suggested ¼ teaspoon of cayenne here, but feel free to up the amount depending on your heat preference. Play ball!

1 cup water

1 cup raw cashews

2 tablespoons white vinegar

¼ teaspoon cayenne powder

½ cup unsweetened plant-based milk

¼ cup Low-Sodium Vegetable Broth (page 136) or store-bought

1 (14.5-ounce) can cannellini or Great Northern white beans, drained and rinsed

3 tablespoons nutritional yeast

¼ cup diced onion

3 garlic cloves, minced

1 (12-ounce) package frozen riced cauliflower

1 recipe Shredded Tofu Meaty Crumbles (page 146) (optional)

Salt (optional)

12 celery stalks, cut into 3-inch-long sticks, for serving

1. Boil the water and put the cashews in a medium bowl. Pour the hot water over the cashews and let soak to soften, at least 15 minutes.

2. Meanwhile, in a small bowl, stir together the vinegar and cayenne. Transfer the cayenne mixture to a blender or food processor, then add the milk, broth, beans, nutritional yeast, onion, and garlic. Drain the cashews and add them to the blender. Blend until creamy.

3. In the slow cooker, combine the cauliflower and tofu crumbles (if using). Season with salt (if using) and cover with the sauce. Mix well to combine. Cover and cook on Low for 2 hours, or until heated through. Serve with the celery sticks for dipping.

Per serving (¼ cup): Calories: 68; Fat: 3g; Carbohydrates: 7g; Protein: 4g; Fiber: 2g; Sodium: 36mg

VARIATION TIP: Replace the cauliflower with two (14.5-ounce) cans of chickpeas, drained, rinsed, and pulsed in the food processor to get a texture similar to shredded chicken.

Gluten-free, Nut-free, Soy-free

Creamy Southwestern Salsa Bean Dip

ABOUT: 12 cups | **PREP TIME:** 10 minutes | **COOK TIME:** 2 hours on High or 4 hours on Low

There's nothing like a nice chunky, cheesy bean dip. This recipe uses both pinto and black beans and adds corn, onion, bell pepper, and tomatoes to create a savory salsa seasoned with the flavors of the Southwest. I can almost picture the sun setting in the Arizona desert when I smell this cooking.

1 medium onion, diced

1 medium green bell pepper, diced

3 garlic cloves, minced

1 (1-pound) bag frozen corn

2 (14.5-ounce) cans no-salt-added diced tomatoes

1 (14.5-ounce) can black beans, drained and rinsed

1 (14.5-ounce) can pinto beans, drained and rinsed

1 tablespoon chili powder

2 teaspoons ground cumin

1 cup Cheeze Sauce (pages 141–143) or store-bought cheeze sauce

Juice of ½ lime

Salt (optional)

Ground black pepper

2 scallions, green and white parts, chopped

¼ cup fresh cilantro, chopped

1. Place the onion, bell pepper, garlic, corn, tomatoes, black beans, pinto beans, chili powder, and cumin in the slow cooker. Cover and cook on High for 2 hours or on Low for 4 hours.

2. During the last 30 minutes of cooking, stir in the cheeze sauce. Before serving, stir in the lime juice and season with salt (if using) and black pepper. Transfer the dip to a bowl, top with the scallions and cilantro, and serve warm.

Per serving (½ cup): Calories: 72; Fat: 1g; Carbohydrates: 14g; Protein: 4g; Fiber: 4g; Sodium: 45mg

LEFTOVERS TIP: Store any leftovers in a container in the refrigerator for up to 5 days. Use the leftovers as a delicious topping for baked potatoes or nachos.

Nut-free, Soy-free

Eggplant Caponata Bruschetta

SERVES: 4 to 8 | **PREP TIME:** 20 minutes | **COOK TIME:** 2 to 3 hours on High or 5 to 6 hours on Low

Caponata is a classic Sicilian recipe, but this one keeps the eggplant unpeeled for a more rustic version that stands up well to slow cooking. For an authentic Italian caponata, use pitted, unstuffed Castelvetrano green olives. Some larger grocery stores offer olive bars, so you can also experiment with different kinds—just make sure they are pitted!

1 medium eggplant, unpeeled and chopped

1 medium onion, diced

2 small zucchini, diced

3 celery stalks, diced

4 garlic cloves, minced

1 cup sliced pitted green olives

2 (14.5-ounce) cans diced tomatoes

2 tablespoons capers, drained

¼ cup red wine vinegar

1 tablespoon maple syrup

1 teaspoon dried basil

1 teaspoon dried oregano

Ground black pepper

Salt (optional)

1 long thin loaf crusty whole-grain bread

3 tablespoons chopped fresh flat-leaf parsley

1. Put the eggplant, onion, zucchini, celery, garlic, and olives in the slow cooker. Pour in the tomatoes. Add the capers, vinegar, maple syrup, basil, oregano, pepper, and salt (if using). Stir well to combine. Cover and cook on High for 2 to 3 hours or on Low for 5 to 6 hours.

2. Preheat the oven to 375°F. Slice the bread into ½-inch slices and place them on a baking sheet. Toast in the oven, keeping an eye on the bread so it doesn't burn. Flip the bread and toast the other side to make it into crostini.

3. After the caponata finishes cooking, stir in the parsley. Spoon about 2 tablespoons of caponata onto each piece of crostini and serve immediately.

Per serving: Calories: 405; Fat: 8g; Carbohydrates: 72g; Protein: 14g; Fiber: 11g; Sodium: 1,493mg

INGREDIENT TIP: Although olive oil isn't included on a WFPBSOS diet, olives are considered a whole food, and while they are created using a salty brine, they can be used in moderation for their flavor and healthy fats.

Gluten-free

Sweet 'n' Spicy Crunchy Snack Mix

MAKES: 5½ cups | **PREP TIME:** 5 minutes | **COOK TIME:** 1½ hours on Low

With its combination of sweet, salty, and spicy, this crunchy snack will cover all your cravings. It's super versatile, too. You can use any combination of nuts you enjoy or stick to a single kind of nut (except pistachios, which tend to burn easily). It makes a delicious homemade gift when placed in a glass jar tied with a festive ribbon—just make sure to save some for yourself!

1 cup raw cashews

1 cup raw almonds

1 cup raw pecan halves

1 cup walnuts

½ cup raw pepitas

½ cup raw sunflower seeds

¼ cup aquafaba (see page 10)

¼ cup maple syrup

1 teaspoon miso paste

1 teaspoon garlic powder

1 teaspoon paprika

2 teaspoons ground ginger

1. Put the cashews, almonds, pecans, walnuts, pepitas, and sunflower seeds in the slow cooker.

2. In a deep bowl, whisk or use an immersion blender to beat the aquafaba until foamy, about 1 minute. Add the maple syrup, miso paste, garlic powder, paprika, and ginger and whisk or blend to combine. Pour over the nuts in the slow cooker and gently toss, making sure all the nuts and seeds are coated.

3. Stretch a clean dish towel or several layers of paper towels over the top of the slow cooker, but not touching the food, and place the lid on top. Cook on Low for 1½ hours, stirring every 20 to 30 minutes to keep the nuts from burning. After each stir, dry any condensation under the lid and replace the towels before re-covering.

4. Line a rimmed baking sheet with parchment paper. Transfer the snack mix to the baking sheet to cool. Store in an airtight container for up to 2 weeks.

Per serving (¼ cup): Calories: 182; Fat: 16g; Carbohydrates: 8g; Protein: 5g; Fiber: 2g; Sodium: 12mg

VARIATION TIP: Swap out the garlic powder and paprika with ground cinnamon and nutmeg and add ½ teaspoon of vanilla extract. Or substitute 1 tablespoon of low-sodium soy sauce for the miso paste and replace the paprika with Chinese five-spice powder.

Gluten-free, Nut-free, Soy-free, Freezable

Crispy Chickpea Snackers

MAKES: 7 to 8 cups | **PREP TIME:** 10 minutes | **COOK TIME:** 4 to 6 hours on High or 8 to 10 hours on Low

There's something special about slow cooker heat on chickpeas that makes them extra crunchy without burning, which can happen far too easily in the oven. These can be a protein-filled afternoon snack, an alternative to croutons on salad, or the crunchy topping on soups such as Curried Zucchini Soup (page 63) or Golden Split Pea Soup (page 67). You can easily scale this recipe down. I make mine in a 1.5-quart slow cooker and divide the recipe by four.

4 (14.5-ounce) cans chickpeas, drained and rinsed

Juice of 2 lemons

1 tablespoon garlic powder

1 tablespoon onion powder

2 teaspoons paprika

Salt (optional)

1. Put the chickpeas into the slow cooker. Add the lemon juice, garlic powder, onion powder, and paprika. Season with salt (if using). Toss gently to thoroughly coat every chickpea with the seasoning.

2. Cover the slow cooker and, using a wooden spoon or a chopstick, prop open the lid to allow the steam to escape. Cook on High for 4 to 6 hours or on Low for 8 to 10 hours, stirring every 30 to 45 minutes to keep the chickpeas from burning.

Per serving (¼ cup): Calories: 56; Fat: 1g; Carbohydrates: 9g; Protein: 3g; Fiber: 3g; Sodium: 81mg

LEFTOVERS TIP: Allow chickpeas to cool completely before placing them in a plastic container or glass jar. Do not cover tightly; leave the lid slightly open to retain crispness. They will keep for 4 to 5 days at room temperature or frozen in an airtight container for up to 1 month.

VARIATION TIP: For Indian-influenced flavor, use lime juice instead of lemon, reduce the garlic and onion powders to 2 teaspoons each, and add 1 teaspoon each of curry powder, turmeric, and cumin. For a sweet snack, use 3 tablespoons maple syrup instead of lemon juice; eliminate the garlic powder, onion powder, and paprika; and add 2 teaspoons of ground cinnamon, 1 teaspoon of ground nutmeg, and 1 teaspoon of ground ginger.

Gluten-free, Nut-free, Soy-free

Spiced Glazed Carrots

SERVES: 4 to 6 | **PREP TIME:** 10 minutes | **COOK TIME:** 2 to 3 hours on High or 4 to 6 hours on Low

Snack staple baby carrots become a delicious hot appetizer with this recipe. Apricot preserves and warming spices like cinnamon, nutmeg, and ginger plus turmeric combine with sweet, tangy orange juice to form a glaze that will make your taste buds happy. Thyme adds a nice citrusy, herbaceous note. Serve them with little toothpicks to avoid sticky fingers.

- 2 pounds fresh baby carrots or frozen cut carrots
- ⅓ cup no-sugar-added apricot preserves, such as Polaner All Fruit brand
- 2 tablespoons orange juice

- 1 tablespoon balsamic vinegar
- 1 tablespoon maple syrup
- ¼ teaspoon ground cinnamon
- ¼ teaspoon ground nutmeg

- ¼ teaspoon ground turmeric
- ½ teaspoon ground ginger
- 1 teaspoon dried thyme
- 1 tablespoon cornstarch
- 2 tablespoons water

1. Place the carrots into the slow cooker. In a measuring cup or medium bowl, stir together the apricot preserves, orange juice, vinegar, maple syrup, cinnamon, nutmeg, turmeric, ginger, and thyme. Pour the sauce into the slow cooker and stir to coat the carrots. Cover and cook on High for 2 to 3 hours or on Low for 4 to 6 hours.

2. During the last 30 minutes of cooking, add the cornstarch and water to a small lidded jar. Cover and shake the jar well to form a slurry and pour it into the slow cooker, stirring occasionally to thicken the sauce and form a glaze.

Per serving: Calories: 175; Fat: <1g; Carbohydrates: 43g; Protein: 2g; Fiber: 7g; Sodium: 179mg

VARIATION TIP: All-fruit preserves are made with whole fruits and their juices, with no added sugars. You can try mango or peach preserves for different flavors. If you can eat sugar, choose any type of fruit preserves, jelly, or jam you prefer.

Gluten-free, Nut-free, Soy-free

Classic Italian Mushrooms

SERVES: 4 to 6 | **PREP TIME:** 10 minutes | **COOK TIME:** 2 hours on Low

Growing up in my Italian mother's kitchen, for much of my life I didn't know there was any other way to prepare mushrooms than with onions, garlic, and parsley sautéed on the stovetop. Keeping the smaller and medium mushrooms whole and serving them with toothpicks turns a side dish into a tasty and oh-so-easy appetizer.

2 pounds white button mushrooms, stemmed

4 garlic cloves, minced

1 medium onion, sliced into half-moons

3 to 5 tablespoons Low-Sodium Vegetable Broth (page 136) or store-bought

3 teaspoons Italian seasoning

Ground black pepper

Salt (optional)

1. Cut any extra-large mushrooms in half. Place the mushrooms in the slow cooker. Add the garlic and onion.

2. Pour in the broth and sprinkle with the Italian seasoning. Season with black pepper and salt (if using). Stir to combine. Cover and cook on Low for 2 hours, or until the mushrooms are cooked through.

Per serving: Calories: 68; Fat: 1g; Carbohydrates: 12g; Protein: 8g; Fiber: 3g; Sodium: 14mg

INGREDIENT TIP: To clean the mushrooms, I rinse mine in a colander under cold water. Other cooks suggest using a wet cloth to wipe away any soil residue, but I find that to be both tedious and less effective than a good quick rinse and then patting them dry with paper towels.

Gluten-free, Nut-free, Soy-free

Cheezy Stuffed Potato Skins

MAKES: 8 potato skins | **PREP TIME:** 20 minutes | **COOK TIME:** 3 to 4 hours on High or 7 to 8 hours on Low, plus 3 to 5 minutes for broiling

When I was a teenager, one of my family's favorite restaurant appetizers was loaded potato skins. In this recipe, instead of discarding the interior of the potato, you'll use it as part of the filling. You'll then toast the skins under the broiler, fill them, and top them with fresh scallions. If your diet allows, try topping these with ½ cup of plant-based sour cream and ½ cup of plant-based bacon crumbles.

4 large russet potatoes (about 2 pounds), unpeeled

1 cup Cheeze Sauce (pages 141–143) or store-bought cheeze sauce, divided

3 tablespoons unsweetened plant-based milk

¾ teaspoon ground black pepper

Salt (optional)

4 scallions, green and white parts, chopped, for serving

1. With a fork, pierce the potatoes on all sides, 10 to 12 times each. Tightly wrap each potato in aluminum foil and place in the slow cooker. Cover and cook on High for 3 to 4 hours or on Low for 7 to 8 hours, until the potatoes are soft and a fork easily slides in and out. Carefully remove the potatoes from the slow cooker and remove the foil. They will be hot!

2. Halve the potatoes lengthwise. Into a small bowl, carefully scoop out the potato from the skins, leaving about ¼ inch around the edges to keep a firm shape.

3. Line a baking sheet with foil. Place the potato skins cut-side up on the baking sheet and broil for 3 to 5 minutes while you prepare the filling.

4. To the bowl with the potato, add ½ cup of the cheeze sauce and the milk, mixing until well combined. Season with pepper and salt (if using).

5. Remove the potato skins from the oven and fill each with the potato mixture. Drizzle about 1 tablespoon of the remaining cheeze sauce over each potato half and sprinkle with the scallions. Serve.

Per serving (1 potato skin): Calories: 177; Fat: 2g; Carbohydrates: 37g; Protein: 6g; Fiber: 3g; Sodium: 26mg

COOKING TIP: Use the method in step 1 to make the fluffiest baked potatoes. Sure, you could bake your potatoes in a microwave or an oven, but I hope you'll give them a try in your slow cooker. Because of the humidity and moist baking environment, the potatoes come out fluffier than any other baking method I've used. You'll love them!

INGREDIENT TIP: Make sure to scrub the potatoes well under running water because you will be eating the skins. Pat them dry before preparing them.

CHAPTER FOUR

Sides

Rosemary-and-Garlic Beet
Salad with Walnuts and
Dijon-Maple Dressing
46

Roasted Red Pepper and
Romaine Salad with Green
Olives and Tomatoes
48

Savory Slow Cooker Stuffing
49

Cajun-Style Red
Beans and Rice
50

Ginger, Shiitake, Pecan,
and Apricot Pilaf
51

Chili-Lime Corn
52

Teriyaki Mushrooms
53

Garlic Mashed Potatoes
54

Maple-Glazed Butternut Squash
and Brussels Sprouts
with Dates and Pecans
55

Chickpea of the Sea Salad
56

Gluten-free, Soy-free

Rosemary-and-Garlic Beet Salad with Walnuts and Dijon-Maple Dressing

SERVES: 4 to 6 | **PREP TIME:** 15 minutes | **COOK TIME:** 3 to 4 hours on High or 4 to 6 hours on Low

When I want to impress a luncheon guest, I whip up this surprisingly simple salad, which can be served as a side dish or paired with a soup like Golden Split Pea Soup (page 67) and crusty bread to make a meal. After the beets are cooked, all that's left is the quick assembly—just be careful because beets can stain!

FOR THE SALAD

2 large red or golden beets (about ½ pound)

3 garlic cloves, crushed

1 fresh rosemary sprig

1 (5-ounce) package fresh arugula

2 tablespoons raw sunflower seed kernels

¼ cup currants

¼ cup chopped walnuts (optional)

FOR THE DRESSING

3 tablespoons balsamic vinegar

1 tablespoon Dijon mustard

1 tablespoon maple syrup

Ground black pepper

Salt (optional)

1. Make the salad: Rinse the beets, dry them with a paper towel, and cut off and discard the stem end. Pierce each beet 10 to 12 times with a fork.

2. Lay a large piece of aluminum foil on your prep surface. Place the beets and garlic on the foil. Cut the rosemary sprig into several pieces and add to the beets. Pull up all sides of the foil, enclosing everything into a packet that is gathered and twisted on top.

3. Place the packet into the slow cooker, cover, and cook for 3 to 4 hours on High or 4 to 6 hours on Low, depending on the size of your beets. Test for doneness by carefully opening the packet and piercing the beets with a fork or paring knife. It should easily slide in.

4. When done, use tongs or a fork to gently remove the beets from the foil. Once cool enough to handle, rub the beets with a paper towel to remove the skins. Slice the peeled beets into bite-size chunks and place into a large bowl.

5. Discard the rosemary. Mince the garlic and add it to the bowl, then add the arugula, sunflower seeds, currants, and walnuts (if using).

6. Make the dressing: In a small jar with a lid, combine the vinegar, Dijon mustard, and maple syrup. Shake until well blended. Pour the dressing over the salad and toss. Season with pepper and salt (if using).

Per serving: Calories: 94; Fat: 3g; Carbohydrates: 15g; Protein: 3g; Fiber: 3g; Sodium: 148mg

Gluten-free, Nut-free, Soy-free

Roasted Red Pepper and Romaine Salad with Green Olives and Tomatoes

PREP TIME: 10 minutes | **COOK TIME:** 2½ to 3 hours on Low

Roasting your own red peppers couldn't be any easier when you use a slow cooker. When added to salads like this one, or stirred into sauces or even blended into Oil-Free Hummus (page 144), they make any dish sing. Here, the sweetness of the peppers combines wonderfully with the salty tang of the olives to give this simple salad complex flavors and textures that come together in a snap after the peppers are cooked.

FOR THE SALAD

- 2 medium red bell peppers, quartered
- 2 hearts romaine lettuce
- ½ pint grape or cherry tomatoes
- 1 (5.6-ounce) jar green olives, drained

FOR THE DRESSING

- 4 tablespoons red wine vinegar
- 2 tablespoons Dijon mustard
- 1 tablespoon maple syrup
- 1 teaspoon lemon juice
- ¾ teaspoon Italian seasoning

1. **Make the salad:** Place the bell peppers in the slow cooker. Cover and cook on Low for 2½ to 3 hours. Carefully remove the peppers. When they are cool enough to handle, peel off the skins and discard. Use a paring knife to get them started (although the skins will likely be falling off). Slice the peppers into ½-inch-wide strips.

2. While the peppers cool, chop the romaine and place it in a large bowl. Cut the tomatoes in half and add them to the bowl. Add the olives and the cooked and peeled peppers.

3. **Make the dressing:** In a small jar with a lid, combine the vinegar, mustard, maple syrup, lemon juice, and Italian seasoning. Tightly close the lid and shake vigorously to blend the dressing well. Pour over the salad and toss well before serving.

Per serving: Calories: 85; Fat: 4g; Carbohydrates: 12g; Protein: 2g; Fiber: 3g; Sodium: 500mg

Nut-free, Soy-free

Savory Slow Cooker Stuffing

SERVES: 5 to 7 | **PREP TIME:** 20 minutes | **COOK TIME:** 45 minutes on High, then 3 to 4 hours on Low

I don't often call for precooking ingredients, but in this case, sautéing the onions, celery, and mushrooms with the seasonings before mixing them with the bread gives this dish that good old-fashioned stuffing flavor from Thanksgivings past. Use plain premade stuffing cubes or a loaf of bread sliced into cubes and left out for a day or two to avoid salt and hidden sugar.

Nonstick cooking spray (optional)

2 (12-ounce) packages stuffing cubes (about 12 cups)

2 tablespoons ground flaxseed

5 tablespoons water

2 small or 1 large onion, diced (about 2 cups)

6 large celery stalks, diced (about 2 cups)

1 (8-ounce) package white button mushrooms, diced

2 teaspoons dried sage

1 teaspoon poultry seasoning

1 teaspoon marjoram

1 teaspoon crushed or ground fennel seed

⅓ cup chopped fresh parsley

Ground black pepper

Salt (optional)

3½ to 5 cups Low-Sodium Vegetable Broth (page 136) or store-bought, divided

1. Coat the inside of the slow cooker with cooking spray (if using) or line it with a slow cooker liner. Place the dry stuffing cubes in the slow cooker. In a small bowl, stir together the flaxseed and water to make 2 flax eggs. Set aside.

2. In a cast-iron or nonstick skillet over medium-high heat, dry sauté the onions, celery, and mushrooms for 5 to 7 minutes, or until the onions are translucent, adding a splash of water or broth to avoid sticking. Stir in the sage, poultry seasoning, marjoram, fennel seed, parsley, pepper, and salt (if using) and cook for another minute or so. Transfer the mixture to the slow cooker and add 3½ cups of broth, stirring to combine. Add more broth, ½ cup at a time, to achieve your desired consistency.

3. Cover and cook on High for 45 minutes, then turn the heat to Low and cook for 3 to 4 hours, until the stuffing reaches the consistency you prefer. Add more broth as needed during the cooking time for a moister stuffing.

Per serving: Calories: 523; Fat: 7g; Carbohydrates: 77g; Protein: 20g; Fiber: 10g; Sodium: 1,715mg

Gluten-free, Nut-free, Soy-free

Cajun-Style Red Beans and Rice

SERVES: 4 to 6 | **PREP TIME:** 15 minutes | **COOK TIME:** 2 hours on High or 3 to 5 hours on Low

In Louisiana, red beans and rice is a staple, and after you make this dish, it may just become a staple in your kitchen, too. Add a mixed green salad, and you've got a complete meal packed with protein and fiber. This recipe has a kick to it, so feel free to use fewer chipotles in adobo or less cayenne to suit your preferences.

1 medium green bell pepper, diced

1 medium onion, diced

2 celery stalks, diced

4 garlic cloves, minced

1 (14.5-ounce) can light or dark red kidney beans, drained and rinsed

1½ cups brown rice

4 to 6 Chipotle Peppers in Adobo Sauce (page 148) or store-bought, finely chopped

3 cups Low-Sodium Vegetable Broth (page 136) or store-bought

2 teaspoons smoked paprika

1 teaspoon ground cumin

1 teaspoon chili powder

½ teaspoon cayenne powder

Ground black pepper

Salt (optional)

1. Put the bell pepper, onion, celery, garlic, beans, and rice in the slow cooker. Add the chipotle peppers, scraping the sauce from the cutting board into the cooker. Add the broth, paprika, cumin, chili powder, and cayenne. Season with black pepper and salt (if using).

2. Cover and cook on High for 2 hours or on Low for 3 to 5 hours, until the liquid is absorbed and the rice is tender. Store leftovers in the refrigerator for up to 4 days.

Per serving: Calories: 366; Fat: 4g; Carbohydrates: 75g; Protein: 14g; Fiber: 11g; Sodium: 315g

INGREDIENT TIP: Chipotles in adobo are dried, smoked, and rehydrated jalapeño peppers that are usually canned in a tangy tomato and ancho chile pepper sauce. They lend the essential smokiness to this dish. While you can find them in the Mexican section of the grocery store, the canned variety often has sugar, oil, and lots of salt, so give the recipe on page 148 a try.

Gluten-free

Ginger, Shiitake, Pecan, and Apricot Pilaf

SERVES: 4 to 6 | **PREP TIME:** 15 minutes | **COOK TIME:** 3 hours on High or 5 to 6 hours on Low

Wild rice is not technically a rice at all. It's a grass with an edible grain that grows in marshy areas. Wild rice triples in size when it cooks, so this recipe will feed a crowd as a side dish. Its dark color will turn everything a similar hue, so be sure to add parsley at the end to punch up the freshness and color.

1 small onion, diced

2 celery stalks, diced

2 carrots, diced

1 cup wild rice

2 cups brown rice

1 (1-inch) piece fresh ginger, peeled and minced, or 1 teaspoon ground ginger

1 teaspoon garlic powder

6 cups Low-Sodium Vegetable Broth (page 136) or store-bought

1 tablespoon low-sodium soy sauce, tamari, or coconut aminos

4 ounces of shiitake mushrooms, stemmed

1 cup chopped pecans

½ cup chopped dried apricots

½ bunch flat-leaf parsley, coarsely chopped

1. Put the onion, celery, and carrots in the slow cooker. Add the wild rice, brown rice, ginger, garlic powder, broth, and soy sauce.

2. Slice the mushroom caps into strips and add to the slow cooker. Stir to combine. Cover and cook on High for 3 hours or on Low for 5 to 6 hours, until all of the liquid is absorbed. Fluff with a fork and top with the pecans, apricots, and parsley to serve.

Per serving: Calories: 757; Fat: 24g; Carbohydrates: 126g; Protein: 19g; Fiber: 15g; Sodium: 216mg

INGREDIENT TIP: Shiitake mushrooms come fresh or dried. If you use dried, you only need 1 to 2 ounces. To rehydrate before cooking, cover them with boiling water and soak for 15 minutes. Use the soaking liquid as part of your 6 cups of broth to add even more flavor.

VARIATION TIP: Try button or cremini mushrooms; omit the wild rice and use all brown rice; change the dried fruit; and change or omit the nuts to suit your dietary needs.

Gluten-free, Nut-free, Soy-free, Freezable

Chili-Lime Corn

SERVES: 4 to 6 | **PREP TIME:** 10 minutes | **COOK TIME:** 3 hours on Low

In my opinion, corn doesn't get enough attention on its own as a side dish, and that's such a shame because it is so delicious and can be enjoyed year-round if you use frozen corn. In this super easy preparation, the garlic, cumin, and tangy lime juice and zest emphasize the sweetness of the corn. While this dish is delicious warm, you can also chill it and use it as a corn salsa on top of Portobello Mushroom Fajitas (page 105) or Southwestern Quinoa Taco Bowls (page 112).

4½ cups frozen corn

1 small red onion, diced

1 small green bell
    pepper, diced

Juice and zest
    of 2 limes

2 teaspoons
    chili powder

1 teaspoon
    ground cumin

1 teaspoon
    garlic powder

Salt (optional)

1. Put the corn, onion, bell pepper, lime juice and zest, chili powder, cumin, garlic powder, and salt (if using) in the slow cooker. Stir to combine.

2. Cover and cook on Low for 3 hours. Refrigerate leftovers in an airtight container for 3 to 4 days or freeze for up to 1 month, and reheat in the microwave.

Per serving: Calories: 188; Fat: 2g; Carbohydrates: 44g; Protein: 7g; Fiber: 7g; Sodium: 47mg

VARIATION TIP: Using this simple recipe, you can also create a yummy corn queso dip by adding 2 cups of Cheeze Sauce (pages 141–143). Or chill the finished dish and stir in one (15-ounce) can of no-salt-added chopped tomatoes with green chiles for a great salsa.

Nut-free

Teriyaki Mushrooms

SERVES: 4 to 6 | **PREP TIME:** 15 minutes | **COOK TIME:** 2 hours on High
or 4 hours on Low

I can't even see the word "teriyaki" without craving the sticky, sweet, tangy sauce, and then I have to make it that same day. Luckily, these ingredients are all in my pantry at any given time so I can make this dish whenever I want. This recipe makes a good bit of sauce, which I like to serve spooned over cooked brown rice with the mushrooms on top.

2 (8-ounce) packages whole cremini mushrooms

½ cup low-sodium soy sauce, tamari, or coconut aminos

¼ cup maple syrup

2 tablespoons rice vinegar

2 garlic cloves, minced

1 piece (1-inch) fresh ginger, peeled and minced, or 1 teaspoon ground ginger

2 tablespoons sesame seeds, divided

2 scallions, green and white parts, chopped, for serving

1. Put the mushrooms in the slow cooker.

2. In a measuring cup or medium bowl, combine the soy sauce, maple syrup, rice vinegar, garlic, and ginger. Pour the sauce over the mushrooms and sprinkle with 1 tablespoon of sesame seeds. Cover and cook on High for 2 hours or on Low for 4 hours.

3. Serve the mushrooms garnished with the scallions and the remaining 1 tablespoon of sesame seeds.

Per serving: Calories: 129; Fat: 3g; Carbohydrates: 21g; Protein: 7g; Fiber: 2g; Sodium: 1,160mg

VARIATION TIP: For a thicker sauce, create a slurry with 1½ tablespoons of cornstarch mixed well with 3 tablespoons of water. Pour the mixture into the slow cooker during the final 30 minutes of cooking. If cooking on Low, increase the temperature to High. Stir the mushrooms frequently. Initially the sauce will take on a whitish color, but when the sauce comes to a boil, it will become clear and thick.

Gluten-free, Nut-free, Soy-free

Garlic Mashed Potatoes

SERVES: 4 to 6 | **PREP TIME:** 15 minutes | **COOK TIME:** 3 to 4 hours on High or 8 hours on Low

If comfort food is supposed to make you feel good, cooking it should also be easy and stress-free. Mashed potatoes are the ultimate in comfort foods, and when made in the slow cooker, you can enjoy them no matter how busy you are or how full your stovetop is. The garlic adds an extra layer of flavor to the finished mashed potatoes, which would be delicious on a holiday or any day of the week for no occasion at all.

6 russet potatoes (about 3 pounds), peeled

1 cup Low-Sodium Vegetable Broth (page 136) or store-bought

1 cup unsweetened plant-based milk, plus more for mashing

5 to 6 garlic cloves, minced

Ground black pepper

Salt (optional)

1. Chop the potatoes into 1- to 2-inch cubes. Put the potatoes in the slow cooker. Pour in the broth.

2. Cover and cook on High for 3 to 4 hours or on Low for 8 hours, until the potatoes are very soft and easily mashed.

3. Add the milk and garlic and mash until your desired consistency is reached. You may need to add up to ½ cup more milk, depending on your preference. Season generously with pepper and salt (if using) and serve.

Per serving: Calories: 286; Fat: 1g; Carbohydrates: 64g; Protein: 8g; Fiber: 5g; Sodium: 65mg

VARIATION TIP: For creamier mashed potatoes, add up to 1 cup of plant-based sour cream, about 4 ounces of plant-based cream cheeze, or up to ½ cup of homemade Cheeze Sauce (pages 141–143).

Gluten-Free, Soy-Free

Maple-Glazed Butternut Squash and Brussels Sprouts with Dates and Pecans

SERVES: 4 to 6 | **PREP TIME:** 15 minutes | **COOK TIME:** 2 to 2½ hours on High or 4 to 6 hours on Low

Depending on how you prepare them, Brussels sprouts can be bitter and have a funky smell, which leads a lot of people to avoid them—but both of those problems disappear with this recipe. Coating the vegetables in a glaze of maple syrup, warm cinnamon, and tangy apple cider vinegar brings out the natural sweetness in the butternut squash and mellows the sprouts. Topping them with the dates and pecans just before serving adds even more sweetness and a crunchy texture.

1 medium butternut squash (about 2 to 3 pounds), peeled, seeded, and cut into 1-inch cubes

¾ pound Brussels sprouts, halved

¼ cup apple cider vinegar

2 tablespoons maple syrup

½ teaspoon ground cinnamon

Ground black pepper

Salt (optional)

1 cup chopped pecans

4 to 5 Medjool dates, pitted and chopped

1. Put the butternut squash and Brussels sprouts in the slow cooker. Cover and cook on High for 2 to 2½ hours or on Low for 4 to 6 hours, checking for doneness each hour, until the squash is tender but not mushy and the Brussels sprouts still have some texture.

2. In a measuring cup or medium bowl, make the glaze by stirring together the vinegar, maple syrup, and cinnamon. Pour the mixture over the vegetables and stir gently to coat. Season with pepper and salt (if using). Toss with the pecans and dates and serve immediately.

Per serving: Calories: 372; Fat: 20g; Carbohydrates: 50g; Protein: 7g; Fiber: 12g; Sodium: 29mg

VARIATION TIP: For a less sweet dish, use ¼ cup of balsamic vinegar, 3 tablespoons of Dijon mustard, and 1 tablespoon of maple syrup. You can replace the dates with raisins, currants, or dried apricots. Change the pecans to walnuts, or to make this dish nut-free, replace the pecans with raw unsalted sunflower seeds or pepitas.

Gluten-free, Nut-free, Soy-free

Chickpea of the Sea Salad

SERVES: 3 to 4 | **PREP TIME:** 15 minutes | **COOK TIME:** 4 hours on High or 8 to 9 hours on Low

This mock tuna salad is great as a sandwich on lightly toasted bread with lettuce, and when served alongside a bowl of your favorite soup (like the Comforting Tomato Soup on page 60), it makes a delicious and satisfying meal. I call for dried chickpeas here because they yield a better overall texture and save a little money. You'll have lots of leftover chickpeas, so freeze them according to the chart on page 152, or use them to make Chickpea Noodle Soup (page 65) or Crispy Chickpea Snackers (page 39).

1 (1-pound) bag dried chickpeas, rinsed and sorted to remove small stones and debris

7 cups water

¼ teaspoon baking soda

5 tablespoons plant-based mayonnaise

1 tablespoon yellow mustard

¼ cup diced dill pickles

¼ cup finely diced onions

1 celery stalk, diced

2 tablespoons rice vinegar

½ teaspoon kelp powder

Ground black pepper

Salt (optional)

1. Put the chickpeas, water, and baking soda in the slow cooker. Cover and cook on High for 4 hours or on Low for 8 to 9 hours. Strain and discard the liquid.

2. Transfer 2 cups of the cooked chickpeas to a food processor and pulse 5 to 10 times to break them up but not turn them to mush. Transfer the pulsed chickpeas to a medium bowl. Save the remaining chickpeas for another recipe.

3. Add the mayonnaise, mustard, pickles, onions, celery, vinegar, kelp powder, pepper, and salt (if using). Stir well to form a salad and chill until serving.

Per serving: Calories: 313; Fat: 21g; Carbohydrates: 25g; Protein: 8g; Fiber: 7g; Sodium: 637mg

INGREDIENT TIP: You can find kelp powder in a health food store, the spice section of a larger grocery store, an Asian market, or online. Or make your own by grinding any dried seaweed product (such as kombu; see page 138) into a powder.

VARIATION TIP: You can easily make your own oil-free mayo. Drain 1 package of silken tofu and blend with 1 tablespoon of lemon juice, 1 teaspoon of Dijon mustard, and ½ teaspoon of nutritional yeast. Add up to 1 additional tablespoon of lemon juice to achieve the tang you prefer. Store it in a jar in the refrigerator for up to 10 days.

CHAPTER FIVE

Soups, Stews, and Chilis

Comforting Tomato Soup
60

Spicy Black Bean Soup
61

Potato-Leek Soup
62

Curried Zucchini Soup
63

French Onion Soup
64

Chickpea Noodle Soup
65

Golden Split Pea Soup
67

Thai-Inspired Coconut
Cabbage Soup
68

Butternut Squash Soup
70

Minestrone Soup
71

Italian Lentil Soup
72

Kale and White
Bean Soup
73

Lobster-Less Bisque
74

Hot and Sour Soup
76

Cauliflower, Chickpea,
Quinoa, and
Coconut Curry
77

Shiitake, Lemongrass,
and Rice Noodle Pho
78

Hearty Potato, Tomato,
and Green Beans Stufato
80

Creamy Corn Chowder
81

New England No-Clam
Chowder
82

Sweet Potato, Red Beans,
and Lentil Stew
83

Chickpea, Kale,
and Lentil Stew
84

Irish Stout Stew
85

Old-Fashioned
Beefless Stew
86

Deconstructed Stuffed
Pepper Stew
87

Mushroom and
Barley Stew
88

Three Bean and
Barley White Chili
89

Mama's Mighty Meatless
Award-Winning Chili
90

Gluten-free, Nut-free, Soy-free, Freezable

Comforting Tomato Soup

SERVES: 6 to 8 | **PREP TIME:** 15 minutes | **COOK TIME:** 3 to 4 hours on High or 6 to 8 hours on Low

This recipe takes a classic favorite and sneaks in a few surprises to add more nutrients and amp up the flavor. I use white beans to create a silky texture and turmeric for its excellent anti-inflammatory and antioxidant properties. If you're in a hurry, you can skip sautéing the vegetables, but I think it adds a nice depth of flavor.

1 medium onion, chopped

1 medium red bell pepper, chopped

4 garlic cloves, coarsely chopped

2 (28-ounce) cans no-salt-added diced tomatoes

½ cup drained and rinsed canned white beans

2 cups Low-Sodium Vegetable Broth (page 136) or store-bought

2 teaspoons dried basil

1 teaspoon ground turmeric

Ground black pepper

Salt (optional)

5 to 6 fresh basil leaves, for garnish (optional)

1. In a medium skillet over medium-low heat, dry sauté the onion and bell pepper for about 5 minutes, or until the onion is translucent.

2. Transfer the onion and bell pepper to the slow cooker. Add the garlic, tomatoes, beans, broth, dried basil, turmeric, black pepper, and salt (if using). Cover and cook on High for 3 to 4 hours or on Low for 6 to 8 hours.

3. Using an immersion blender or a countertop blender, puree the soup until creamy. Some small foamy bubbles may form on the surface from blending. Use a slower blending speed, allow the bubbles to dissipate for a few minutes before serving, or simply serve it as is. Divide among bowls, top with the fresh basil (if using), and serve.

Per serving: Calories: 113; Fat: <1g; Carbohydrates: 23g; Protein: 4g; Fiber: 7g; Sodium: 42mg

INGREDIENT TIP: Use only red bell peppers. Green peppers are underripe, and we need the sweetness from the fully ripened red pepper as well as the brightness from the color.

Nut-free, Freezable

Spicy Black Bean Soup

SERVES: 4 to 6 | **PREP TIME:** 15 minutes | **COOK TIME:** 3 to 4 hours on High or 7 to 8 hours on Low

Like many Latin-inspired dishes, this soup screams to be served with some delicious toppings, like Greener Guacamole (page 145), chopped fresh cilantro, a lime wedge for squeezing, plant-based sour cream, and plant-based Cheddar shreds. But this flavorful soup will easily stand up on its own, too. According to my Cuban American friend Christina Pint, authentic Cuban black bean soup, which is what inspired this dish, is served either chunky or blended smooth, depending on your personal preference.

1 medium onion, diced

3 garlic cloves, minced

1 carrot, diced

1 celery stalk, diced

2 (14.5-ounce) cans black beans, drained and rinsed

1 Chipotle Pepper in Adobo Sauce (page 148) or store-bought, chopped

1 tablespoon chili powder

1 tablespoon Plant-Based Worcestershire Sauce (page 139) or store-bought

2 tablespoons tomato paste

4 cups Low-Sodium Vegetable Broth (page 136) or store-bought

1 bay leaf

Ground black pepper

Salt (optional)

1. Combine the onion, garlic, carrot, celery, beans, chipotle pepper, chili powder, Worcestershire sauce, tomato paste, broth, bay leaf, black pepper, and salt (if using) in the slow cooker.

2. Cover and cook on High for 3 to 4 hours or on Low for 7 to 8 hours. Remove and discard the bay leaf, and serve.

Per serving: Calories: 265; Fat: 2g; Carbohydrates: 51g; Protein: 15g; Fiber: 19g; Sodium: 224mg

Gluten-free, Soy-free, Freezable

Potato-Leek Soup

SERVES: 6 to 8 | **PREP TIME:** 15 minutes | **COOK TIME:** 3 to 4 hours on High
or 7 to 8 hours on Low

Leeks, a member of the onion family, are sort of a giant scallion. They grow up through the soil, collecting it between all the many layers. To wash a leek, slice it and submerge the pieces in a large bowl of cool water, agitating them slightly. The dirt will fall to the bottom of the bowl, and the leeks will be ready to provide their earthy sweetness to this classic French soup.

6 yellow potatoes (about 2 pounds), unpeeled and cut into 1½-inch cubes

3 leeks, light green and white parts, sliced and rinsed

2 celery stalks, chopped

2 garlic cloves, crushed

½ cup raw cashews

6 cups Low-Sodium Vegetable Broth (page 136) or store-bought

2 teaspoons chopped fresh thyme, or 1 teaspoon dried thyme

1 bay leaf

Ground black pepper

Salt (optional)

¼ to 1 cup unsweetened plant-based milk, for thinning

1. Put the potatoes, leeks, celery, garlic, cashews, broth, thyme, bay leaf, pepper, and salt (if using) in the slow cooker. Cover and cook on High for 3 to 4 hours or on Low for 7 to 8 hours.

2. After cooking, remove and discard the bay leaf. Using an immersion blender or a countertop blender, puree the soup until rich and creamy. If the soup is too thick, add the milk, ¼ cup at a time, until it reaches your preferred consistency.

Per serving: Calories: 221; Fat: 5g; Carbohydrates: 40g; Protein: 7g; Fiber: 4g; Sodium: 65mg

VARIATION TIP: If you can't eat cashews, use a can of white beans (drained and rinsed) to achieve a similar consistency, although you may find you need more milk at the end of the recipe to achieve a creamy mouthfeel.

Gluten-free, Nut-free, Soy-free, Freezable

Curried Zucchini Soup

SERVES: 4 to 6 | **PREP TIME:** 10 minutes | **COOK TIME:** 3 to 4 hours on High or 6 to 7 hours on Low

Simple, spicy, smooth—it doesn't get much easier or better than this soup! When you've got more zucchini growing in your garden than you know what to do with, or you've found some at the farmers' market or grocery store when it's in season, this soup is a great way to prepare this versatile summer squash. Feel free to hold back on the amount of curry powder if you're not a fan of heavy spiciness.

1 medium
onion, chopped

3 garlic cloves, minced

3 medium zucchini
(about 1½ pounds),
chopped into
1-inch pieces

2 yellow potatoes
(about ⅔ pounds),
unpeeled and
chopped

5 cups Low-Sodium
Vegetable Broth
(page 136) or
store-bought

1 tablespoon
curry powder

Ground black pepper

Salt (optional)

1. Put the onion, garlic, zucchini, potatoes, broth, curry powder, pepper, and salt (if using) in the slow cooker. Cover and cook on High for 3 to 4 hours or on Low for 6 to 7 hours.

2. Before serving, blend until smooth using an immersion blender or transfer the contents to a blender in batches. Carefully blend, beginning on low and gradually increasing speed to avoid hot soup going all over your kitchen.

Per serving: Calories: 119; Fat: 1g; Carbohydrates: 25g; Protein: 5g; Fiber: 5g; Sodium: 38mg

VARIATION TIP: You can use all summer squashes interchangeably in this recipe. To give the dish an Italian flair, omit the curry powder and add 1 tablespoon of Italian seasoning plus a pinch of red pepper flakes for some heat.

Nut-free, Freezable

French Onion Soup

SERVES: 6 to 8 | **PREP TIME:** 15 minutes | **COOK TIME:** 4 to 5 hours on High
or 8 to 9 hours on Low

I've been making French onion soup since I was a teenager, and I'm thrilled to have developed this plant-based version that's just as good without the cheese. This is a great recipe for any bread that's going stale. If you'd like your bread more fully toasted, you can bake it in a 350°F oven for 5 to 10 minutes while the onions cook.

4 to 6 large onions (about 3 pounds), cut into half-moons

4½ cups Low-Sodium Vegetable Broth (page 136) or store-bought, divided

1½ cups red wine (about half a bottle)

¼ cup Plant-Based Worcestershire Sauce (page 139) or store-bought

2 bay leaves

1 teaspoon dried thyme

Ground black pepper

Salt (optional)

1 loaf crusty whole-grain bread, for serving

1. In a large Dutch oven or an extra deep nonstick skillet over medium heat, dry sauté the onions for about 15 minutes, or until soft and golden brown. Add the broth, 2 tablespoons at a time, as needed to keep the onions from sticking.

2. Transfer the onions to the slow cooker. Add the remaining broth, the wine, Worcestershire sauce, bay leaves, thyme, pepper, and salt (if using). Cover and cook on High for 4 to 5 hours or on Low for 8 to 9 hours. Remove and discard the bay leaves.

3. When there is 5 to 10 minutes left of cooking time, slice the bread into large cubes or rounds to fit your bowls. To serve, place the bread at the bottom of each bowl and ladle the soup over the top.

Per serving: Calories: 343; Fat: 1g; Carbohydrates: 64g; Protein: 10g; Fiber: 7g; Sodium: 550mg

LEFTOVERS TIP: Store the soup (without bread) in the freezer for up to 3 months. To reheat, bring it to a boil and follow step 3 for serving.

VARIATION TIP: For a French onion soup gratiné, place the bread and ladle the soup into ovenproof bowls, top each with up to ¼ cup of plant-based Swiss or mozzarella cheeze, and place under the broiler for 1 to 2 minutes.

Nut-free, Soy-free, Freezable

Chickpea Noodle Soup

SERVES: 6 to 8 | **PREP TIME:** 15 minutes | **COOK TIME:** 2 to 3 hours on High or 5 to 6 hours on Low

Just because you're eating plant-based food, it doesn't mean you have to miss out on any classics, including this noodle soup. Loaded with chickpeas, it's got plenty of protein to fill you up. The noodles cook right in the slow cooker at the end of the cooking time for a truly one-pot meal. Finished with a squeeze of lemon juice and a sprinkle of chopped parsley for brightness, this soup isn't just for sick days.

1 medium onion, diced

3 carrots, diced

3 celery stalks, diced

4 garlic cloves, minced

2 (14.5-ounce) cans chickpeas, drained and rinsed

8 cups Low-Sodium Vegetable Broth (page 136) or store-bought

1 teaspoon dried parsley

1 bay leaf

Ground black pepper

Salt (optional)

10 ounces whole-wheat pasta spirals

Juice of ½ lemon

3 tablespoons chopped fresh parsley

1. Put the onion, carrots, celery, garlic, chickpeas, broth, dried parsley, bay leaf, pepper, and salt (if using) in the slow cooker. Cover and cook on High for 2 to 3 hours or on Low for 5 to 6 hours.

2. In the final 30 minutes of cooking, remove and discard the bay leaf. Add the pasta, stirring well. After 30 minutes, check the pasta for your preferred level of doneness. Remove and discard the bay leaf. Stir in the lemon juice and fresh parsley before serving.

Per serving: Calories: 332; Fat: 4g; Carbohydrates: 64g; Protein: 14g; Fiber: 13g; Sodium: 251mg

LEFTOVERS TIP: If freezing, do not add the pasta noodles until you're ready to serve. Cook the pasta separately according to the package directions, then add it to the reheated soup to serve.

VARIATION TIP: For a more traditional "chicken" noodle soup, try one of the brands of grilled chick'n pieces from the frozen section of your grocery store. Replace half or all the chickpeas with the chick'n pieces (about 3 cups total).

Gluten-free, Nut-free, Soy-free, Freezable

Golden Split Pea Soup

SERVES: 5 to 7 | **PREP TIME:** 10 minutes | **COOK TIME:** 3 to 4 hours on High or 7 to 8 hours on Low

I have a lot of favorite comfort soups, and split pea is at the top of that long list. Usually made with green split peas, this recipe mixes things up and uses yellow split peas, along with other golden ingredients like carrots and turmeric, lending the soup added anti-inflammatory benefits. The cumin imparts a welcome smokiness, while the potato adds great body. Give me a bowl of this soup, a warm blanket, and a comfy spot on the couch (and my remote), and I'm as happy as a pea in a pod!

1 medium onion, diced

3 carrots, diced

3 celery stalks, diced

3 garlic cloves, crushed

1 cup yellow split peas, rinsed and stones removed

1 yellow potato (about ⅓ pounds), unpeeled and cubed

4 cups Low-Sodium Vegetable Broth (page 136) or water

1 bay leaf

¾ teaspoon ground cumin

¾ teaspoon ground turmeric

½ teaspoon dry mustard

Ground black pepper

Salt (optional)

1. Put the onion, carrots, celery, garlic, peas, potato, broth, bay leaf, cumin, turmeric, mustard, pepper, and salt (if using) in the slow cooker. Cover and cook on High for 3 to 4 hours or on Low for 7 to 8 hours.

2. Remove and discard the bay leaf. Using an immersion blender or a countertop blender, fully puree the soup before serving.

Per serving: Calories: 207; Fat: 1g; Carbohydrates: 40g; Protein: 11g; Fiber: 13g; Sodium: 59g

VARIATION TIP: If you can't find yellow split peas, use green split peas. To emphasize the green color, omit the carrots and turmeric and use parsnips and dried thyme instead. Top either version with a dollop of plant-based sour cream for extra creaminess.

Nut-free

Thai-Inspired Coconut Cabbage Soup

SERVES: 4 to 6 | **PREP TIME:** 15 minutes | **COOK TIME:** 3 to 4 hours on High or 7 to 8 hours on Low

This soup is all about the flavorful broth that's made rich and creamy with coconut milk. Extra-firm pressed tofu takes on the fragrant flavors of the lemongrass, ginger, and lime peel, and it provides some protein while the napa cabbage adds some crunch.

1 (16-ounce) package extra-firm tofu

1 lime

2 lemongrass stalks, cut into 3- to 4-inch pieces and crushed

6 cups Low-Sodium Vegetable Broth (page 136) or store-bought

1 (2-inch) piece fresh ginger, peeled and minced, or 1 tablespoon ginger powder

2 carrots, diced

1 large onion, diced

3 garlic cloves, minced

1 teaspoon curry powder

¼ cup Plant-Based Fish Sauce (page 138) or store-bought

Ground black pepper

Salt (optional)

1 (14.5-ounce) can full-fat coconut milk

1 small head napa cabbage, chopped into bite-size pieces (about 4 cups)

½ bunch Thai or regular basil (about 20 to 30 leaves), for serving

1. Drain the tofu. Wrap it in a generous amount of paper towels, and place it on a plate or cutting board. Place the heaviest skillet or pot you own on top, and press out as much liquid from the tofu as possible while you prepare the other ingredients.

2. Using a vegetable peeler, remove and reserve the outer green peel of the lime, taking care not to include the bitter white pith. Juice the lime and cover and refrigerate the juice until just before serving.

3. Put the lime peel, lemongrass, broth, ginger, carrots, onion, garlic, curry powder, fish sauce, pepper, and salt (if using) in the slow cooker.

4. Cube the tofu into ¾-inch pieces and add it to the slow cooker. Cover and cook on High for 3 to 4 hours or on Low for 7 to 8 hours.

5. In the last 30 minutes of cooking, remove and discard the lemongrass and lime peel. Stir in the coconut milk and cabbage. Just before serving, add the reserved lime juice. Top each serving with a few torn basil leaves.

Per serving: Calories: 369; Fat: 25g; Carbohydrates: 26g; Protein: 16g; Fiber: 6g; Sodium: 500mg

INGREDIENT TIP: You can find lemongrass in the produce department of your grocery store or in Asian markets. To crush it, bend the pieces with your hands.

Gluten-free, Nut-free, Soy-free, Freezable

Butternut Squash Soup

SERVES: 5 to 7 | **PREP TIME:** 15 minutes | **COOK TIME:** 3 to 4 hours on High or 7 to 8 hours on Low

Don't let the funky shape of this winter squash scare you away. Butternut squash is easy to manage, or you can find it already cut into pieces in the fresh produce or frozen foods section of your grocery store, making the prep for this recipe a breeze. The finished soup gets its sweetness from the butternut squash and is made simply with just a few supporting ingredients. When I ask my teenage daughters what kind of soup they want, they often request this one.

1 medium onion, diced

1 large carrot, diced

1 celery stalk, diced

1 Yukon Gold potato, unpeeled, diced

1 medium butternut squash (2 to 3 pounds), peeled, seeded, and diced

5 cups Low-Sodium Vegetable Broth (page 136) or water, or enough to cover

1 bay leaf

1 teaspoon dried thyme

Ground black pepper

Salt (optional)

1. Put the onion, carrot, celery, potato, and squash in the slow cooker. Add the broth until the vegetables are just submerged. (Depending on the size of the squash, you may need more or less than 5 cups.) Add the bay leaf, thyme, pepper, and salt (if using). Cover and cook on High for 3 to 4 hours or on Low for 7 to 8 hours.

2. Remove and discard the bay leaf. Using an immersion blender or a countertop blender, fully puree the soup before serving.

Per serving: Calories: 101; Fat: <1g; Carbohydrates: 25g; Protein: 3g; Fiber: 6g; Sodium: 39mg

Nut-free, Soy-free, Freezable

Minestrone Soup

SERVES: 4 to 6 | **PREP TIME:** 15 minutes | **COOK TIME:** 3 to 4 hours on High or 7 to 8 hours on Low

There must be as many variations of minestrone soup as there are Italian grandparents in the world. This hearty vegetable soup has a tomato-based broth with any combination of vegetables. With the addition of a small pasta at the end, it makes for a filling meal, especially when you pair it with a nice piece of crusty whole-grain bread.

1 medium onion, diced

1 large carrot, diced

1 large celery stalk, diced

4 garlic cloves, minced

1 cup fresh or frozen cut green beans

1 (15-ounce) can chickpeas, drained and rinsed

1 (15-ounce) can white beans, drained and rinsed , rinsed and sorted

1 (28-ounce) can diced no-salt-added tomatoes

8 cups Low-Sodium Vegetable Broth (page 136) or store-bought

1 tablespoon Italian seasoning

Ground black pepper

Salt (optional)

1 medium zucchini, diced

2 cups baby spinach leaves

1 cup small whole-wheat pasta, such as elbow

Juice of 1 lemon

Fresh basil leaves, for garnish (optional)

1. Put the onion, carrot, celery, garlic, green beans, chickpeas, beans, tomatoes, broth, Italian seasoning, pepper, and salt (if using) in the slow cooker. Cover and cook on High for 3 to 4 hours or on Low for 7 to 8 hours.

2. In the last 30 minutes of cooking, add the zucchini, spinach, and pasta, stirring well to incorporate. Just before serving, stir in the lemon juice. Garnish with torn basil leaves (if using).

Per serving: Calories: 436; Fat: 4g; Carbohydrates: 85g; Protein: 20g; Fiber: 23g; Sodium: 244mg

LEFTOVERS TIP: If freezing, do not add the pasta until you are ready to serve. Cook it separately according to the package directions and add it to the soup before serving.

VARIATION TIP: Start with the base of onions, garlic, broth, and tomatoes, and use your favorite vegetables, beans, and greens. Instead of pasta, add a couple of diced potatoes in step 1.

Gluten-free, Nut-free, Soy-free, Freezable

Italian Lentil Soup

SERVES: 6 to 8 | **PREP TIME:** 10 minutes | **COOK TIME:** 3 to 4 hours on High or 7 to 8 hours on Low

Here's another soup reminiscent of my childhood. Simply known as lentil soup in my family, it was often served as a simple meal with a large loaf of crusty bread on Friday evenings during Lent, when Catholics abstain from eating meat. The lentils are full of satisfying fiber and protein, and the colorful vegetables lend a rainbow of nutrients perfect for any occasion.

1 medium onion, diced

3 garlic cloves, minced

2 carrots, diced

2 celery stalks, diced

1 pound (about 2⅓ cups) dried green or brown lentils, rinsed and sorted

1 (28-ounce) can no-salt-added crushed tomatoes

8 cups Low-Sodium Vegetable Broth (page 136) or store-bought

1 tablespoon Italian seasoning

Ground black pepper

Salt (optional)

1. Put the onion, garlic, carrots, celery, lentils, tomatoes, broth, Italian seasoning, pepper, and salt (if using) in the slow cooker.

2. Cover and cook on High for 3 to 4 hours or on Low for 7 to 8 hours.

Per serving: Calories: 354; Fat: 1g; Carbohydrates: 67g; Protein: 20g; Fiber: 34g; Sodium: 309mg

INGREDIENT TIP: There are three kinds of readily available lentils: green, brown, and red. Green and brown lentils can be used interchangeably, but red lentils are smaller and cook in about half the time. As a variation on this recipe, try a pound of red lentils in place of the brown or green and start testing for doneness after cooking for 2 hours on High or 5 hours on Low. One final type of lentils are black lentils, which are tiny and often used as a plant-based caviar. Don't use those here.

Gluten-free, Nut-free, Soy-free, Freezable

Kale and White Bean Soup

SERVES: 4 to 6 | **PREP TIME:** 10 minutes | **COOK TIME:** 2 to 3 hours on High or 4 to 5 hours on Low

My grandmom used to make this as escarole soup for my mom when she was growing up, and later my mom made it on special occasions, always with mini meatballs (see the variation tip). Escarole isn't usually available where I live, so Tuscan or green curly kale makes a perfect easy-to-find alternative for this fresh and simple soup.

2 medium shallots, finely diced

3 garlic cloves, minced

2 (14.5-ounce) cans white beans, drained and rinsed

1 pound fresh Tuscan or curly kale (about 5 large stalks), chopped

6 cups Low-Sodium Vegetable Broth (page 136) or store-bought

Ground black pepper

Salt (optional)

½ bunch fresh flat-leaf parsley, chopped

1. Put the shallots, garlic, beans, kale, broth, pepper, and salt (if using) in the slow cooker.

2. Cover and cook on High for 2 to 3 hours or on Low for 4 to 5 hours. Stir in the parsley just before serving.

Per serving: Calories: 233; Fat: 2g; Carbohydrates: 42g; Protein: 13g; Fiber: 12g; Sodium: 112mg

VARIATION TIP: Turn this recipe into Italian wedding soup by adding frozen Italian meatless meatballs, such as Gardein brand, at the beginning of cooking. Top the soup with a sprinkle of Plant-Based Parmesan (page 137). Escarole, curly endive, or other bitter greens can be used in place of the kale.

Nut-free

Lobster-Less Bisque

SERVES: 4 to 6 | **PREP TIME:** 20 minutes | **COOK TIME:** 2 to 3 hours on High or 5 to 6 hours on Low

Each year at Christmastime, my dad made a delicious lobster bisque. When I asked him for the recipe, I was surprised to see it was mostly canned soups mixed with heavy cream. This plant-based update is healthier and every bit as decadent and delicious. On special occasions, drizzle on a teaspoon or two of sherry to each adult's serving.

1 (14.5-ounce) can no-salt-added crushed tomatoes

1 teaspoon white vinegar or white wine vinegar

3 tablespoons Plant-Based Fish Sauce (page 138) or store-bought

1 tablespoon Plant-Based Worcestershire Sauce (page 139) or store-bought

1 tablespoon miso paste

2 teaspoons Old Bay seasoning

1 teaspoon paprika

Ground black pepper

Salt (optional)

3 bay leaves

1 large shallot, finely diced

3 cups Low-Sodium Vegetable Broth (page 136) or store-bought, divided

6 garlic cloves, minced

¼ cup tapioca starch or cornstarch

½ cup white wine

1 (15-ounce) can no-salt-added tomato sauce

8 hearts of palm, drained, rinsed, and chopped, divided

1 (14.5-ounce) can full-fat coconut milk

1. In the slow cooker, whisk together the tomatoes, vinegar, fish sauce, Worcestershire sauce, miso paste, Old Bay seasoning, paprika, pepper, and salt (if using). Add the bay leaves.

2. Heat a medium skillet over medium-high heat and dry sauté the shallot for 3 to 4 minutes, until translucent. Add the broth, 1 to 2 tablespoons at a time, as necessary to avoid sticking. Add the garlic and sauté for another 30 seconds, until fragrant. Sprinkle the tapioca starch over the shallot and garlic, stirring to combine. Whisk in the wine until a thick sauce forms. Whisk in the tomato sauce.

3. Transfer the mixture to the slow cooker, add the remaining broth, and whisk well. Cover and cook on High for 2 to 3 hours or on Low for 5 to 6 hours. In the final 30 minutes of cooking, remove and discard the bay leaves and stir in the hearts of palm (reserving about 2 tablespoons for garnish). Add the coconut milk and stir until fully incorporated.

4. After cooking, spoon the soup into bowls and top with the remaining 2 tablespoons of hearts of palm.

Per serving: Calories: 376; Fat: 19g; Carbohydrates: 44g; Protein: 9g; Fiber: 9g; Sodium: 1,239mg

VARIATION TIP: Lobster mushrooms or hen-of-the-woods mushrooms also work well here. If using, add to the soup in step 1 and omit the hearts of palm.

Nut-free

Hot and Sour Soup

SERVES: 6 to 8 | **PREP TIME:** 15 minutes | **COOK TIME:** 3 to 4 hours on High
or 7 to 8 hours on Low

When you need to clear your sinuses, hot and sour soup will certainly do the trick.
The "hot" part comes from the spicy and slightly floral white pepper as well as the
red pepper, while the "sour" part comes from the vinegar. Adding a small amount of
cornstarch slurry at the end allows the soup to thicken ever so slightly and gives it an
irresistible glossy sheen.

6 ounces shiitake
mushrooms, sliced

1 (8-ounce) can sliced
bamboo shoots

4 garlic cloves, minced

1 (2-inch) piece fresh
ginger, peeled
and minced

1 (16-ounce) package
extra-firm tofu,
drained and cut into
bite-size cubes

8 cups Low-Sodium
Vegetable Broth
(page 136) or
store-bought

¼ cup low-sodium
soy sauce, tamari, or
coconut aminos

¼ cup rice vinegar

½ teaspoon ground
white pepper

½ teaspoon red
pepper flakes

3 baby bok choy,
chopped into
bite-size pieces

2 tablespoons
cornstarch

¼ cup water

4 scallions, green and
white parts, chopped,
for serving

½ bunch cilantro,
chopped, for serving

1. Put the mushrooms, bamboo shoots, garlic, ginger, tofu, broth, soy sauce, vinegar,
white pepper, and red pepper flakes in the slow cooker. Cover and cook on High for
3 to 4 hours or on Low for 7 to 8 hours.

2. In the last 30 minutes of cooking, add the bok choy. In a small bowl, whisk together
the cornstarch and water. Add the slurry to the slow cooker and stir well to incorporate. To serve, ladle the soup into bowls and top each with the scallions and cilantro.

Per serving: Calories: 138; Fat: 5g; Carbohydrates: 14g; Protein: 11g; Fiber: 4g; Sodium: 420mg

INGREDIENT TIP: White pepper is a traditional ingredient for this dish, so don't swap it
out. You can find it in the spice aisle of most grocery stores or in an Asian market. Ground
white pepper works here, or you can try crushing whole peppercorns with a mortar and
pestle, with a peppermill, or in a sturdy bowl with the back of a metal spoon. Change the
amount, depending on your threshold for heat.

Gluten-free, Nut-free, Soy-free

Cauliflower, Chickpea, Quinoa, and Coconut Curry

SERVES: 5 to 7 | **PREP TIME:** 15 minutes | **COOK TIME:** 3 to 4 hours on High or 7 to 8 hours on Low

At the request of my editor, I developed this curry, which has a heavenly aroma while it cooks and a beautiful golden color when finished. Incorporating grain from the quinoa, fiber and protein from the chickpeas, starch from the sweet potato, and the cruciferous cauliflower, this creamy dish feels decadent and is a meal on its own.

- 1 head cauliflower, cut into bite-size pieces (about 4 cups)
- 1 medium onion, diced
- 3 garlic cloves, minced
- 1 medium sweet potato (about ⅓ pound), peeled and diced
- 1 (14.5-ounce) can chickpeas, drained and rinsed
- 1 (28-ounce) can no-salt-added diced tomatoes

- ¼ cup Low-Sodium Vegetable Broth (page 136) or store-bought
- ¼ cup quinoa, rinsed
- 2 (15-ounce) cans full-fat coconut milk
- 1 (1-inch) piece fresh ginger, peeled and minced
- 2 teaspoons ground turmeric

- 2 teaspoons garam masala
- 1 teaspoon ground cumin
- 1 teaspoon curry powder
- Ground black pepper
- Salt (optional)
- ½ bunch cilantro, coarsely chopped (optional)

1. Put the cauliflower, onion, garlic, sweet potato, chickpeas, tomatoes, broth, quinoa, coconut milk, ginger, turmeric, garam masala, cumin, curry powder, pepper, and salt (if using) in the slow cooker.

2. Cover and cook on High for 3 to 4 hours or on Low for 7 to 8 hours. At the end of cooking, stir in the cilantro (if using), reserving a couple of tablespoons to garnish each dish.

Per serving: Calories: 503; Fat: 32g; Carbohydrates: 48g; Protein: 11g; Fiber: 12g; Sodium: 195mg

INGREDIENT TIP: Garam masala is a common and popular ground spice blend in Indian, Pakistani, and Afghani cuisine. "Garam" means hot and "masala" means spices. You can find it in most grocery stores in the spice aisle.

Nut-free, Freezable

Shiitake, Lemongrass, and Rice Noodle Pho

SERVES: 6 to 8 | **PREP TIME:** 20 minutes | **COOK TIME:** 8 to 10 hours on Low

The secret to this delicious Vietnamese-style pho is the fragrant broth that's simmered for hours with multiple spices. It might look like an overwhelming ingredient list, but it's so worth it. The fresh toppings added at the end lend brightness and texture. Serve them family-style so your guests can add them to their soup as they prefer.

FOR THE SPICE BUNDLE

1 teaspoon black peppercorns

1 teaspoon fennel seeds

1 teaspoon cardamom pods

3 whole cloves

FOR THE SOUP

1 medium onion, quartered

3 garlic cloves, crushed

2 star anise pods

1 (3-inch) piece fresh ginger, unpeeled and sliced into large pieces

1 cinnamon stick

3 lemongrass stalks, cut into 3-inch chunks and crushed

6 dried shiitake mushrooms

8 cups Low-Sodium Vegetable Broth (page 136) or store-bought

3 tablespoons low-sodium soy sauce, tamari, or coconut aminos

Salt (optional)

8 cups water

1 (16-ounce) package rice noodles

FOR THE TOPPINGS

2 cups fresh bean sprouts

1 bunch scallions (about 6 or 7), green and white parts, chopped

1 bunch cilantro, coarsely chopped

2 limes, cut into wedges

1 bunch Thai basil

1. Make the spice bundle: Put the peppercorns, fennel, cardamom, and cloves in a tea strainer or piece of cheesecloth. If using cheesecloth, tie the ingredients into a bundle with kitchen twine. Place the spice bundle in the slow cooker.

2. Make the soup: Add the onion, garlic, star anise, ginger, cinnamon stick, lemongrass, mushrooms, broth, and soy sauce to the slow cooker. Season with salt (if using). Cover and cook on Low for 8 to 10 hours.

3. About 20 minutes before the cooking time ends, boil the water. Place the rice noodles in a large deep bowl and cover them with the boiling water to soften them. Gently stir the noodles every few minutes. After 8 minutes, begin tasting them for your preferred doneness. Drain the noodles and portion into individual bowls.

4. When the broth is finished, remove the spice bundle and discard the contents. With a slotted spoon, remove the mushrooms, slice them, and set aside. Remove and discard all remaining solids. Return the sliced mushrooms to the broth.

5. When ready to serve, plate the bean sprouts, scallions, cilantro, lime wedges, and basil. Ladle the soup over the noodles and allow each person to top their soup however they prefer.

Per serving: Calories: 421; Fat: 1g; Carbohydrates: 96g; Protein: 11g; Fiber: 8g; Sodium: 458mg

LEFTOVERS TIP: You can store the strained broth (without noodles) in the freezer for up to 3 months. When you're ready to use the pho broth, bring it to a boil and continue from step 3 to add the softened noodles and fresh mix-ins at the end.

Gluten-free, Nut-free, Soy-free, Freezable

Hearty Potato, Tomato, and Green Beans Stufato

SERVES: 4 to 6 | **PREP TIME:** 10 minutes | **COOK TIME:** 3 to 4 hours on High or 6 to 7 hours on Low

Stufato is Italian for "stew," and I enjoyed this dish frequently when I was growing up, usually in the summertime when green beans are plentiful and inexpensive. It was always served with a nice, crusty loaf of bread to sop up the flavorful tomato sauce. Just smelling it cooking brings me back to my childhood.

1 large onion, chopped

4 garlic cloves, minced

3 red or yellow potatoes (about 1 pound), unpeeled and cut into 1- to 2-inch chunks

1 pound fresh or frozen green beans, cut into bite-size pieces

1 (28-ounce) can no-salt-added crushed tomatoes

2 teaspoons dried oregano

2 teaspoons dried basil

1 teaspoon dried rosemary

½ teaspoon red pepper flakes (optional)

Ground black pepper

Salt (optional)

Chopped fresh parsley, for garnish (optional)

1. Put the onion, garlic, potatoes, green beans, tomatoes, oregano, basil, rosemary, red pepper flakes (if using), pepper, and salt (if using) in the slow cooker.

2. Cover and cook on High for 3 to 4 hours or on Low for 6 to 7 hours, until the potatoes are fork tender. Serve garnished with parsley (if using).

Per serving: Calories: 197; Fat: 1g; Carbohydrates: 40g; Protein: 8g; Fiber: 9g; Sodium: 30mg

VARIATION TIP: There are two ways to make this an even more fulfilling meal: include a pound of white button mushrooms for a meaty addition, or try one of the many plant-based Italian sausage brands on the market. Simply chop the mushrooms or sausage (or both!) into bite-size pieces and add them to the slow cooker with the rest of the ingredients.

Gluten-Free, Nut-free, Freezable

Creamy Corn Chowder

SERVES: 4 to 6 | **PREP TIME:** 15 minutes | **COOK TIME:** 3 to 4 hours on High or 7 to 8 hours on Low

This recipe was inspired by my friend Chef Brian Rodgers, the father of plant-based BBQ and what he calls "mountain grub." He posted this recipe on his Next Thing Smokin Foundation Facebook page, and I adapted it for the slow cooker, adding a few of my own tweaks with Brian's approval. This soup works equally well with corn cut fresh from the cob or frozen corn (which is what I almost always use for convenience).

1 large onion, diced

4 garlic cloves, minced

4 cups fresh or frozen corn

4 yellow potatoes (about 1⅓ pounds), unpeeled and diced

6 cups Low-Sodium Vegetable Broth (page 136) or store-bought

1 teaspoon garlic powder

½ teaspoon dried basil

½ teaspoon dried thyme

Ground black pepper

Salt (optional)

3 tablespoons chickpea flour

1 (14.5-ounce) can white beans, drained and rinsed

1 tablespoon miso paste

1. Put the onion, garlic, corn, potatoes, broth, garlic powder, basil, thyme, pepper, and salt (if using) in the slow cooker. Cover and cook on High for 3 to 4 hours or on Low for 7 to 8 hours.

2. In the last 30 minutes of cooking, remove 3 cups of soup and blend in a blender or food processor with the chickpea flour, beans, and miso paste until a thick and creamy consistency is achieved. Return the blended mixture to the slow cooker and stir to combine. Serve hot.

Per serving: Calories: 410; Fat: 2g; Carbohydrates: 88g; Protein: 17g; Fiber: 16g; Sodium: 191mg

INGREDIENT TIP: Chickpea flour is ground raw or roasted chickpeas. Bob's Red Mill makes chickpea flour that is sold in most grocery stores, or you can make your own with a high-speed blender by grinding raw dried chickpeas into a fine flour. You can use white whole-wheat flour, if needed.

Nut-free

New England No-Clam Chowder

SERVES: 6 to 8 | **PREP TIME:** 20 minutes | **COOK TIME:** 3 to 4 hours on High
or 7 to 8 hours on Low

In my opinion, the best chowders are thick, rich, and creamy with good body, approaching the thickness of a stew. That's just what this recipe delivers. Loaded with protein from the chickpea flour and the beans pureed and mixed in at the end, this chowder also has lots of filling fiber.

¼ cup chickpea flour (see page 81)

4 yellow potatoes (about 1⅓ pounds), unpeeled and cut into 1½-inch cubes

1 medium onion, diced

2 garlic cloves, minced

3 celery stalks, diced

4 ounces shiitake or other mushrooms, diced

4½ cups Low-Sodium Vegetable Broth (page 136) or store-bought

¼ cup white wine

3 tablespoons Plant-Based Fish Sauce (page 138) or store-bought

1 teaspoon dried thyme

2 bay leaves

⅓ teaspoon celery seed

Ground black pepper

Salt (optional)

1 (14.5-ounce) can white beans, drained and rinsed

½ cup unsweetened plant-based milk

1. Place the chickpea flour and potatoes in a gallon-size resealable bag and shake well to coat.

2. Transfer the floured potatoes to the slow cooker. Add the onion, garlic, celery, mushrooms, broth, wine, fish sauce, thyme, bay leaves, celery seed, and pepper. Season with salt (if using). Cover and cook on High for 3 to 4 hours or on Low for 7 to 8 hours.

3. In the last 30 minutes of cooking, blend together the beans and milk until smooth. Add the bean mixture to the soup and mix well to combine. The chowder should be thick and creamy. Remove and discard the bay leaves before serving.

Per serving: Calories: 208; Fat: 1g; Carbohydrates: 41g; Protein: 9g; Fiber: 9g; Sodium: 263mg

Gluten-free, Nut-free, Soy-free, Freezable

Sweet Potato, Red Beans, and Lentil Stew

SERVES: 5 to 7 | **PREP TIME:** 15 minutes | **COOK TIME:** 3 to 4 hours on High or 7 to 8 hours on Low

My dad used to make a pot roast with sweet potatoes and orange juice concentrate, which was the inspiration for this hearty stew. Filled with fiber and protein from the beans and lentils, and lightly sweetened with orange juice (I promise it's worth the extra 2 to 3 minutes to squeeze the oranges yourself!), this dish is filling and delicious.

¼ cup chickpea flour (see page 81)

4 medium sweet potatoes (about 1½ pounds), peeled and cut into 1½-inch cubes

1 medium onion, diced

1 garlic clove, minced

1 (14.5-ounce) can red kidney beans, drained and rinsed

1 cup dried brown or green lentils, rinsed and sorted

4½ cups Low-Sodium Vegetable Broth (page 136) or store-bought

1 cup orange juice (from 2 to 3 oranges)

1 teaspoon dried oregano

½ teaspoon celery seed

Ground black pepper

Salt (optional)

1. Place the chickpea flour and sweet potatoes in a gallon-size resealable bag and shake well to coat.

2. Transfer the floured potatoes to the slow cooker. Add the onion, garlic, beans, lentils, broth, orange juice, oregano, celery seed, and pepper. Season with salt (if using).

3. Cover and cook on High for 3 to 4 hours or on Low for 7 to 8 hours.

Per serving: Calories: 396; Fat: 2g; Carbohydrates: 78g; Protein: 18g; Fiber: 24g; Sodium: 209mg

Gluten-free, Nut-free, Soy-free, Freezable

Chickpea, Kale, and Lentil Stew

SERVES: 4 to 6 | **PREP TIME:** 15 minutes | **COOK TIME:** 3 to 4 hours on High or 6 to 8 hours on Low

Also known as harira, this stew uses warming spices like cinnamon, cumin, and fresh ginger, which are classic to Moroccan cooking. The kale is a less traditional addition, but the hearty greens turn the dish into a complete meal. It's filled with protein and fiber, and it will fill up even the hungriest folks at your table. I serve this stew topped with a plant-based plain yogurt and some chopped almonds, with a lemon wedge on the side for squeezing.

1 medium onion, diced

2 celery stalks, diced

5 garlic cloves, minced

4 ounces kale (about 5 or 6 large leaves), chopped

½ cup chopped fresh parsley, divided

1 (1-inch) piece fresh ginger, peeled and minced, or 2 teaspoons ground ginger

1 (14.5-ounce) can chickpeas, drained and rinsed

1 cup dried brown or green lentils, rinsed and sorted

1 (28-ounce) can no-salt-added crushed tomatoes

7 cups Low-Sodium Vegetable Broth (page 136) or store-bought

2 teaspoons paprika

1 teaspoon ground coriander

1 teaspoon ground cumin

½ teaspoon ground cinnamon

¼ teaspoon red pepper flakes

Ground black pepper

Salt (optional)

Juice from ½ lemon

1. Put the onion, celery, garlic, kale, ¼ cup of parsley, the ginger, chickpeas, lentils, tomatoes, broth, paprika, coriander, cumin, cinnamon, red pepper flakes, black pepper, and salt (if using) in the slow cooker. Cover and cook on High for 3 to 4 hours or on Low for 6 to 8 hours.

2. Just before serving, stir in the remaining ¼ cup of parsley and the lemon juice.

Per serving: Calories: 398; Fat: 3g; Carbohydrates: 69g; Protein: 22g; Fiber: 31g; Sodium: 206mg

INGREDIENT TIP: Parsley lends its distinctive earthy and slightly peppery flavor to the dish as it cooks and is added again just before serving to brighten the stew. I prefer flat-leaf parsley, which has a more pronounced flavor.

Nut-free, Freezable

Irish Stout Stew

SERVES: 4 to 6 | **PREP TIME:** 15 minutes | **COOK TIME:** 3 to 4 hours on High or 7 to 8 hours on Low

The Irish stout in this recipe gives this stew a richness and depth of flavor you won't get any other way. After hours of cooking, any alcohol evaporates, leaving behind a malty flavor with hints of chocolate. To thicken, the potatoes are coated with chickpea flour that will slowly release into the stew as it cooks. Finishing the stew with the cabbage in the last half hour of cooking provides a nice textural element.

1 medium onion, diced

3 carrots, diced

3 celery stalks, diced

1 parsnip, diced

3 garlic cloves, minced

1 pound whole white button or cremini mushrooms

¼ cup chickpea flour (see page 81)

4 russet potatoes (about 2 pounds), peeled and chopped into 1-inch pieces

4 cups Low-Sodium Vegetable Broth (page 136) or store-bought

1 (10- to 14-ounce can or bottle) Irish stout beer, such as Guinness

1 tablespoon tomato paste

2 tablespoons Plant-Based Worcestershire Sauce (page 139) or store-bought

1 tablespoon dried thyme

1 bay leaf

Ground black pepper

Salt (optional)

Small head savoy or green cabbage, chopped (about 7 cups)

1. Put the onion, carrots, celery, parsnip, garlic, and mushrooms in the slow cooker.

2. Place the chickpea flour and potatoes in a gallon-size resealable bag and shake well to coat. Transfer the floured potatoes to the slow cooker.

3. Add the broth, beer, tomato paste, Worcestershire sauce, thyme, bay leaf, pepper, and salt (if using) to the slow cooker. Stir well to combine. Cover and cook on High for 3 to 4 hours or on Low for 7 to 8 hours, stirring occasionally to avoid sticking.

4. In the final 30 minutes of cooking, remove and discard the bay leaf, add the cabbage, and stir well. Serve hot.

Per serving: Calories: 399; Fat: 2g; Carbohydrates: 81g; Protein: 17g; Fiber: 16g; Sodium: 351mg

Nut-free, Freezable

Old-Fashioned Beefless Stew

SERVES: 4 to 6 | **PREP TIME:** 20 minutes | **COOK TIME:** 3 to 4 hours on High or 7 to 8 hours on Low

Did your parents have a go-to dish they made when you were growing up? Mine did, and it was beef stew. The vegetables were always cut larger because the stewing meat was usually tough and had to cook for a long time. In this recipe, I replace the beef with meaty mushrooms, and I call for the vegetables to be cut larger for a heartier finished dish.

⅓ cup chickpea flour (see page 81)

4 red potatoes (about 1⅓ pounds), unpeeled and cut into 1-inch chunks

1 large onion, diced

4 carrots, cut into 1-inch chunks

4 celery stalks, cut into 1-inch chunks

1 pound whole white button or cremini mushrooms

6 cups Low-Sodium Vegetable Broth (page 136) or store-bought

2 tablespoons Plant-Based Worcestershire Sauce (page 139) or store-bought

2 tablespoons tomato paste

3 bay leaves

2 teaspoons dried thyme

2 teaspoons garlic powder

Ground black pepper

Salt (optional)

1. Place the chickpea flour and potatoes in a gallon-size resealable bag and shake well to coat. Transfer the floured potatoes to the slow cooker.

2. Add the onion, carrots, celery, mushrooms, broth, Worcestershire sauce, tomato paste, bay leaves, thyme, garlic powder, pepper, and salt (if using) to the slow cooker and stir to combine.

3. Cover and cook on High for 3 to 4 hours or on Low for 7 to 8 hours, stirring occasionally to prevent the stew from sticking. Remove and discard the bay leaves before serving.

Per serving: Calories: 290; Fat: 2g; Carbohydrates: 62g; Protein: 12g; Fiber: 11g; Sodium: 331mg

VARIATION TIP: Try parsnips, turnips, or celery root in place of or in addition to the vegetables in this recipe. Substitute frozen plant-based grilled steak chunks for the mushrooms. Finally, if you feel the stew isn't as thick as you would like, mix a tablespoon or two of chickpea flour, whole-wheat flour, or cornstarch with about ¼ cup of water and stir it into your stew to reach your desired consistency. Allow the stew to cook for a few minutes longer to eliminate the raw-flour taste.

Gluten-free, Nut-free, Soy-free, Freezable

Deconstructed Stuffed Pepper Stew

SERVES: 6 to 8 | **PREP TIME:** 15 minutes | **COOK TIME:** 4 to 5 hours on Low

Here's another recipe to thank my editor for! When she asked me to include a stuffed pepper recipe, I knew the prep time for actual stuffed peppers wouldn't be practical: cooking the vegetables, rice, and lentils separately, then stuffing the peppers, and then topping them with the sauce. Enter this stuffed pepper stew recipe, which incorporates all of the same yummy ingredients in a hearty, stick-to-your-ribs one-pot dish.

1 medium onion, diced

1 medium red bell pepper, diced

1 medium green bell pepper, diced

2 celery stalks, diced

1 cup brown rice

1 cup dried green or brown lentils, rinsed and sorted

1 (14.5-ounce) can no-salt-added diced tomatoes

1 (8-ounce) can tomato sauce

4 cups Low-Sodium Vegetable Broth (page 136) or store-bought

1 tablespoon maple syrup or Date Syrup (page 134)

1 tablespoon Italian seasoning

Ground black pepper

Salt (optional)

1. Put the onion, red bell pepper, green bell pepper, celery, rice, lentils, tomatoes, tomato sauce, broth, syrup, Italian seasoning, black pepper, and salt (if using) in the slow cooker. Stir to combine, then cover and cook on Low for 4 to 5 hours.

2. After 2 hours, stir to avoid sticking. Then stir every 30 minutes until the rice and lentils are cooked through.

Per serving: Calories: 284; Fat: 2g; Carbohydrates: 59g; Protein: 11g; Fiber: 18g; Sodium: 226mg

Nut-free, Freezable

Mushroom and Barley Stew

SERVES: 4 to 6 | **PREP TIME:** 15 minutes | **COOK TIME:** 3 to 4 hours on High or 7 to 8 hours on Low

Hearty, earthy, filling, and flavorful are the words that come to mind when I think of this tasty mushroom and barley stew. The humble ingredients come together to form a dish that I can hardly wait to make when fall temps start to get cooler and I'm craving an easy bowl full of something yummy.

1 medium onion, diced

3 garlic cloves, minced

3 carrots, diced

3 celery stalks, diced

1 pound white button mushrooms, quartered

1 cup pearl barley

8 cups Low-Sodium Vegetable Broth (page 136) or store-bought

2 tablespoons Plant-Based Worcestershire Sauce (page 139) or store-bought

2 bay leaves

1 teaspoon dried thyme

Ground black pepper

Salt (optional)

1. Put the onion, garlic, carrots, celery, mushrooms, barley, broth, Worcestershire sauce, bay leaves, thyme, pepper, and salt (if using) in the slow cooker.

2. Cover and cook on High for 3 to 4 hours or on Low for 7 to 8 hours. Remove and discard the bay leaves before serving.

Per serving: Calories: 295; Fat: 1g; Carbohydrates: 63g; Protein: 11g; Fiber: 11g; Sodium: 276mg

VARIATION TIP: Add your favorite leafy green, such as fresh baby spinach or Swiss chard, in the last 15 to 20 minutes of cooking to make this stew a full meal. You could also add a cup or so of frozen or fresh broccoli florets in the last two hours of cooking.

Nut-free, Soy-free, Freezable

Three Bean and Barley White Chili

SERVES: 4 to 6 | **PREP TIME:** 15 minutes | **COOK TIME:** 3 to 4 hours on High or 7 to 8 hours on Low

The first time I made this chili, my husband and I were on an autumn camping trip with friends in the glorious Smoky Mountains. I knew chili would be perfect for our group potluck, but another friend was making a red chili, and that's how this recipe was born. You can use navy, cannellini, or Great Northern beans. It's amazing with a big dollop of Greener Guacamole (page 145) and a few drops of your favorite hot sauce and topped with chopped scallions and cilantro. If you're not following the WFPB diet, you might want to add some plant-based Cheddar cheeze or sour cream.

1 large onion, diced

5 garlic cloves, minced

1 medium green bell pepper, diced

16 ounces frozen corn

1 (4-ounce) can mild diced green chiles

1 (14.5-ounce) can chickpeas, drained and rinsed

1 (14.5-ounce) can white beans, drained and rinsed

1 (14.5-ounce) can black-eyed peas, drained and rinsed

1¼ cups barley

3 tablespoons nutritional yeast

1 tablespoon ground cumin

1 tablespoon chili powder

2 teaspoons dried oregano

Ground black pepper

Salt (optional)

5 cups Low-Sodium Vegetable Broth (page 136) or store-bought

2 cups unsweetened plant-based milk

1. Put the onion, garlic, bell pepper, corn, green chiles, chickpeas, white beans, black-eyed peas, barley, nutritional yeast, cumin, chili powder, oregano, black pepper, salt (if using), broth, and milk in the slow cooker. Stir to combine.

2. Cover and cook on High for 3 to 4 hours or on Low for 7 to 8 hours.

Per serving: Calories: 695; Fat: 8g; Carbohydrates: 132g; Protein: 33g; Fiber: 33g; Sodium: 401mg

Nut-free, Freezable

Mama's Mighty Meatless Award-Winning Chili

SERVES: 4 to 6 | **PREP TIME:** 20 minutes | **COOK TIME:** 3 to 4 hours on High or 7 to 8 hours on Low

Before I began eating plant-based, one of the dishes I was famous for was my award-winning chili. It was delicious, and I wasn't sure I'd ever be able to get close to its flavor again—until I discovered a secret ingredient that gives a similar bite to my original. That ingredient is bulgur wheat, and it's fabulous. Here published for the first time ever is . . . my award-winning meatless chili!

1 (14.5-ounce) can pinto beans, drained and rinsed, divided

2 cups Low-Sodium Vegetable Broth (page 136) or store-bought, divided

1 large onion, diced

1 large green bell pepper, diced

1 large red bell pepper, diced

4 garlic cloves, minced

½ cup bulgur wheat

1 (14.5-ounce) can black beans, drained and rinsed

1 (14.5-ounce) can kidney beans, drained and rinsed

1 (4-ounce) can mild diced green chiles

1 (28-ounce) can no-salt-added diced tomatoes

2 tablespoons chili powder

1 tablespoon cocoa powder

2 teaspoons ground cumin

2 teaspoons garlic powder

1 teaspoon dried oregano

2 tablespoons Plant-Based Worcestershire Sauce (page 139) or store-bought

Ground black pepper

Salt (optional)

1. Put a little more than half of the pinto beans and ¾ cup of broth in a blender. Blend well and set aside.

2. Put the onion, green and red bell peppers, garlic, bulgur wheat, black beans, kidney beans, green chiles, tomatoes, chili powder, cocoa powder, cumin, garlic powder, oregano, Worcestershire sauce, black pepper, and salt (if using) in the slow cooker.

3. Stir in the pinto bean and broth mixture, the remaining pinto beans, and the remaining 1¼ cups of broth. Cover and cook on High for 3 to 4 hours or on Low for 7 to 8 hours.

Per serving: Calories: 491; Fat: 4g; Carbohydrates: 96g; Protein: 24g; Fiber: 27g; Sodium: 734mg

VARIATION TIP: Feel free to experiment. A chopped poblano pepper will add mild heat, while a jalapeño pepper will add even more spice. Mix up the types of canned beans or throw in some frozen corn. You can add store-bought meatless ground-beef-style crumbles or the Shredded Tofu Meaty Crumbles (page 146) in the last hour of cooking.

CHAPTER SIX

Entrées

Tangy Cabbage, Apples,
and Potatoes
94

Black-Eyed Peas
and Collard Greens
with Brown Rice
95

Shiitake Mushroom and
Quinoa Lettuce Wraps
with Peanut Sauce
96

Cheezy Broccoli
and Rice Casserole
98

Green Lentil and
Potato Dal
99

Creamy Orzo with
Wheatberries, Raisins,
and Swiss Chard
100

BBQ Black Beans and
Sweet Potatoes
101

Ratatouille
102

Sweet and Savory
Root Veggies and
Butternut Squash
103

Mushroom
Stroganoff
104

Portobello
Mushroom Fajitas
105

BBQ Pulled Jackfruit
Sandwiches
107

Green Pepper,
Potato, and Mushroom
Scallopini Sandwiches
108

Lentil Sloppy Joes
110

Black Bean, Corn,
and Salsa Fiesta
111

Southwestern Quinoa
Taco Bowls
112

Hawaiian-Inspired
Pepper Pot with
Brown Rice
113

Cajun-Style
Jambalaya
114

Garlic Lovers'
Chili Mac and Cheeze
115

Spinach Lasagna
116

Gluten-free, Nut-free, Soy-free

Tangy Cabbage, Apples, and Potatoes

SERVES: 4 to 6 | **PREP TIME:** 15 minutes | **COOK TIME:** 3 to 4 hours on High or 6 to 8 hours on Low

When German immigrants settled in the hills of central and western Pennsylvania in the 1800s, they brought their faith, their Deutsch (German) language, and their fabulous food. This recipe with potatoes, apples, and cabbage seasoned with warming cinnamon, tangy vinegar and mustard, and fennel is a simple and hearty dish inspired by their cuisine.

6 red or yellow potatoes (about 2 pounds), unpeeled and cut into 1½-inch chunks

½ medium onion, diced

2 apples, peeled, cored, and diced

½ teaspoon ground cinnamon

½ medium head green cabbage, sliced

1 cup Low-Sodium Vegetable Broth (page 136) or store-bought

½ cup apple juice, apple cider, or hard apple cider

2 tablespoons apple cider vinegar

2 teaspoons ground mustard, or 1 tablespoon spicy brown mustard

1 teaspoon fennel seeds

1 bay leaf

Ground black pepper

Salt (optional)

1. In the slow cooker, layer the potatoes, onion, and apples, in that order. Sprinkle the cinnamon over the apples. Top with the cabbage.

2. In a small bowl, whisk together the broth, apple juice, vinegar, mustard, fennel, bay leaf, pepper, and salt (if using). Pour over the cabbage.

3. Cover and cook on High for 3 to 4 hours or on Low for 6 to 8 hours. Remove and discard the bay leaf and serve.

Per serving: Calories: 266; Fat: 1g; Carbohydrates: 62g; Protein: 7g; Fiber: 10g; Sodium: 69mg

VARIATION TIP: For crunchier cabbage, wait to add it until the last 30 to 45 minutes of cooking. Many Bavarian recipes use kielbasa in similar recipes, and there are some good plant-based kielbasa or bratwurst-style sausages on the market now.

Gluten-free, Nut-free, Soy-free

Black-Eyed Peas and Collard Greens with Brown Rice

SERVES: 4 to 6 | **PREP TIME:** 15 minutes | **COOK TIME:** 2 to 3 hours on High or 5 to 6 hours on Low

This Southern dish traditionally served on New Year's Day is great any time of year. It uses black-eyed peas, which aren't peas but are a type of legume, like navy beans or chickpeas. I keep some homemade pepper vinegar (see the ingredient tip) on hand and generously douse my serving of this dish with it.

1 medium onion, diced

4 garlic cloves, minced

2 celery stalks, diced

1 medium green bell pepper, diced

2 (14.5-ounce) cans black-eyed peas, drained and rinsed

1 cup Low-Sodium Vegetable Broth (page 136) or store-bought

4 cups packed chopped collard greens

½ to 1 teaspoon cayenne powder

1 teaspoon smoked paprika

¼ teaspoon dried thyme

1 bay leaf

Ground black pepper

Salt (optional)

2 to 3 cups cooked brown rice, for serving

Hot pepper vinegar or hot sauce, for serving (optional)

1. Put the onion, garlic, celery, bell pepper, black-eyed peas, broth, collard greens, cayenne, paprika, thyme, bay leaf, pepper, and salt (if using) in the slow cooker.

2. Cover and cook on High for 2 to 3 hours or on Low for 5 to 6 hours. Remove and discard the bay leaf.

3. Portion the cooked rice into bowls and spoon the beans and greens over the rice. Drizzle each portion with some pepper vinegar (if using).

Per serving: Calories: 337; Fat: 3g; Carbohydrates: 66g; Protein: 16g; Fiber: 14g; Sodium: 86mg

INGREDIENT TIP: To make your own hot pepper vinegar, put a handful of washed and dried hot peppers into a lidded glass container, cover with white vinegar, and let sit at least overnight—the longer the better. I use tiny Thai chiles because they fit into the mouth of a shaker bottle easily. For extra heat, slice a few of the peppers in half before adding. The vinegar will keep indefinitely at room temperature.

Shiitake Mushroom and Quinoa Lettuce Wraps with Peanut Sauce

SERVES: 4 to 6 | **PREP TIME:** 20 minutes | **COOK TIME:** 2 to 3 hours on High or 5 to 6 hours on Low

This recipe uses quinoa for heartiness, and shiitake mushrooms and water chestnuts combine to give the filling great chewy and crunchy textures. The peanut sauce at the end adds a delicious sweet and salty flavor. Don't skip it: it really makes the wraps.

FOR THE FILLING

2 cups riced cauliflower

½ cup chopped walnuts

4 ounces shiitake mushrooms, diced

1 (8-ounce) can water chestnuts, diced

4 scallions, green and white parts, sliced and separated

3 garlic cloves, minced

1 (1-inch) piece fresh ginger, peeled and minced, or 1 teaspoon ground ginger

1 cup quinoa, rinsed

2 cups Low-Sodium Vegetable Broth (page 136) or store-bought

2 tablespoons rice vinegar

2 tablespoons low-sodium soy sauce, tamari, or coconut aminos

1 tablespoon maple syrup or Date Syrup (page 134)

2 tablespoons sesame seeds

FOR THE PEANUT SAUCE

1 tablespoon maple syrup or Date Syrup (page 134)

1 tablespoon rice vinegar

½ cup no-salt-added creamy peanut butter

¼ to ⅓ cup hot water

½ teaspoon garlic powder

½ teaspoon ground ginger

FOR THE LETTUCE WRAPS

12 to 15 lettuce leaves, such as romaine or butter lettuce

1 cup shredded carrots

1. Make the filling: Put the cauliflower, walnuts, mushrooms, water chestnuts, white parts of the scallions, garlic, ginger, quinoa, broth, rice vinegar, soy sauce, maple syrup, and sesame seeds in the slow cooker. Stir to combine. Cover and cook on High for 2 to 3 hours or on Low for 5 to 6 hours.

2. Make the peanut sauce: Meanwhile, in a small bowl, whisk together the maple syrup, vinegar, peanut butter, hot water, garlic powder, and ginger. Cover and refrigerate until serving. Just before serving, stir in the reserved scallion greens.

3. Assemble the wraps: Scoop about ¼ cup of the filling onto each lettuce leaf and top with the carrots and peanut sauce. Serve.

Per serving: Calories: 607; Fat: 32g; Carbohydrates: 66g; Protein: 21g; Fiber: 13g; Sodium: 357mg

Gluten-free, Nut-free, Soy-free

Cheezy Broccoli and Rice Casserole

SERVES: 6 to 8 | **PREP TIME:** 15 minutes | **COOK TIME:** 2 to 3 hours on High or 6 to 7 hours on Low

Typically for a casserole, you precook the rice and other ingredients and bake them in the casserole dish with the sauce. But for this time-saving, mostly hands-off recipe, you toss all the ingredients except the cheeze sauce into the slow cooker, and they all cook together. The cheeze sauce is stirred in at the end and brings this plant-based version of a casserole classic to life.

Nonstick cooking spray (optional)

1 medium onion, diced

2 crowns and stems of broccoli, diced

2 cups brown rice

4 cups Low-Sodium Vegetable Broth (page 136) or store-bought

8 ounces mushrooms, diced

3 garlic cloves, minced

1 tablespoon nutritional yeast

1 teaspoon dry mustard

Ground black pepper

Salt (optional)

2 cups Cheeze Sauce (pages 141–143) or store-bought cheeze sauce

1. Coat the inside of the slow cooker with cooking spray (if using) or line it with a slow cooker liner.

2. Add the onion, broccoli, rice, broth, mushrooms, garlic, nutritional yeast, mustard, pepper, and salt (if using). Stir well. Cover and cook on High for 2 to 3 hours or on Low for 6 to 7 hours. Stir occasionally in the last hour of cooking to keep the rice from settling and overcooking. In the last 10 minutes of cooking, gently stir in the cheeze sauce. Serve.

Per serving: Calories: 322; Fat: 6g; Carbohydrates: 63g; Protein: 12g; Fiber: 9g; Sodium: 60mg

VARIATION TIP: You could add a frozen plant-based grilled-style chick'n, such as Quorn brand, in place of the mushrooms. For additional texture, add one (8-ounce) can of chopped water chestnuts.

Gluten-free, Nut-free, Soy-free

Green Lentil and Potato Dal

SERVES: 4 to 6 | **PREP TIME:** 15 minutes | **COOK TIME:** 3 to 4 hours on High or 6 to 8 hours on Low

This is Indian-style comfort food at its finest. I use the larger green or brown lentils because they provide a more toothsome texture that stands up to the slow cooker times. With the addition of potatoes, which take on a gorgeous color as they cook, and spinach tossed in at the end, you've got a one-pot meal that's sure to please.

1 cup dried green or brown lentils, rinsed and sorted

3 cups of Low-Sodium Vegetable Broth (page 136) or store-bought

2 large russet potatoes (about 1 pound), peeled and cut into 1½-inch cubes

1 medium onion, diced

4 garlic cloves, minced

1 tablespoon garam masala

1 (1-inch) piece fresh ginger, peeled and minced, or 1 teaspoon ground ginger

1 teaspoon ground turmeric

1 teaspoon ground cumin

Ground black pepper

Salt (optional)

1 (5-ounce) package fresh baby spinach

1. Put the lentils, broth, potatoes, onion, garlic, garam masala, ginger, turmeric, cumin, pepper, and salt (if using) in the slow cooker. Cover and cook on High for 3 to 4 hours or on Low for 6 to 8 hours.

2. In the last 15 minutes of cooking, stir in the spinach to wilt, pushing it down into the rest of the dal. Serve.

Per serving: Calories: 366; Fat: 1g; Carbohydrates: 74g; Protein: 17g; Fiber: 24g; Sodium: 51mg

VARIATION TIP: If you prefer a creamier finish, add ½ to 1 cup of canned full-fat coconut milk. Spice it up with up to 1 tablespoon of curry powder and/or a generous pinch of red pepper flakes.

Nut-free, Soy-free

Creamy Orzo with Wheatberries, Raisins, and Swiss Chard

SERVES: 4 to 6 | **PREP TIME:** 15 minutes | **COOK TIME:** 3 to 4 hours on High or 6 to 8 hours on Low

If wheatberries are not a staple you keep on hand, maybe this recipe and the breakfast recipe for Maple, Apple, and Walnut Great Grains (page 20) will change your mind. I always have this grain in my pantry because it cooks to be toothsome and creamy, similar to barley but with a sweeter flavor. Here we pump up the sweetness with raisins tossed in at the end along with some greens to make this a one-pot meal.

1¼ cup wheatberries	Ground black pepper	½ cup raisins
½ medium onion, diced	Salt (optional)	3 to 4 large stalks Swiss chard, stemmed and chopped
1 garlic clove, minced	1 cup orzo	
5 cups Low-Sodium Vegetable Broth (page 136) or store-bought		

1. Put the wheatberries, onion, garlic, broth, pepper, and salt (if using) in the slow cooker. Stir to combine. Cover and cook on High for 3 to 4 hours or on Low for 6 to 8 hours.

2. In the last 15 minutes of cooking, stir in the orzo, raisins, and Swiss chard. Cook until the orzo is tender and the chard has wilted. Serve hot.

Per serving: Calories: 442; Fat: <1g; Carbohydrates: 95g; Protein: 16g; Fiber: 16g; Sodium: 147mg

INGREDIENT TIP: Orzo is a type of small rice-shaped pasta, but don't mistake it for rice. You'll find orzo in a small package in the pasta section at your grocery store. You could also use any other miniature shaped pasta or even couscous, which will cook in 5 minutes.

VARIATION TIP: Substitute dried cranberries for the raisins and any other kind of leafy green veggie, such as spinach, collard greens, or kale, for the Swiss chard. If you use collards or kale, add them at the beginning of the cooking time.

BBQ Black Beans and Sweet Potatoes

SERVES: 4 to 6 | **PREP TIME:** 15 minutes | **COOK TIME:** 2 to 3 hours on High or 4 to 6 hours on Low

Rustic, flavorful, and quick to prepare thanks to leaving the sweet potatoes unpeeled, this dish is both hearty and economical. If you're not a fan of heavy spiciness, use only one jalapeño pepper, or leave them out entirely and replace the jalapeños with a small diced green bell pepper. Fans of set-your-mouth-on-fire spiciness should take a look at the ingredient tip.

- 3 medium sweet potatoes (around 1 pound), peeled and cut into 1½-inch cubes
- 1 (14.5-ounce) can black beans, drained and rinsed
- 1 medium onion, diced
- 2 jalapeño peppers, finely diced

- ½ cup SOS-Free BBQ Sauce (page 140) or store-bought
- ¼ cup Low-Sodium Vegetable Broth (page 136) or store-bought
- 1 teaspoon ground cumin

- 1 teaspoon chili powder
- 1 teaspoon garlic powder
- Ground black pepper
- Salt (optional)

1. Put the sweet potatoes, beans, onion, jalapeños, BBQ sauce, broth, cumin, chili powder, garlic powder, pepper, and salt (if using) in the slow cooker. Stir to combine.

2. Cover and cook on High for 2 to 3 hours or on Low for 4 to 6 hours.

Per serving: Calories: 219; Fat: 1g; Carbohydrates: 45g; Protein: 8g; Fiber: 12g; Sodium: 258mg

INGREDIENT TIP: The Scoville heat units (SHU) scale measures hotness in peppers. Bell peppers have 0 and jalapeños score between 2,500 and 8,000. If you love spiciness, replace the jalapeño with a serrano (10,000 to 23,000 SHU), a highly spicy habanero (100,000 to 350,000 SHU), or the ultra-hot Scotch bonnet pepper (445,000 SHU).

VARIATION TIP: For a smoky flavor add a few pieces of torn plant-based bacon at the beginning of the cooking time. Or try adding some Shredded Tofu Meaty Crumbles (page 146). You could serve these rolled up in a burrito with a dollop of Greener Guacamole (page 145).

Gluten-free, Nut-free, Soy-free

Ratatouille

SERVES: 4 to 6 | **PREP TIME:** 15 minutes | **COOK TIME:** 2 to 3 hours on High or 4 to 6 hours on Low

Not all French food is laden with heavy cream and butter—enter ratatouille. This popular dish from the Provence region in France is similar in ingredients to the Eggplant Caponata Bruschetta (page 37), but ratatouille is considered a meal while caponata is more of a relish. Serve it on its own or over rice, quinoa, mashed potatoes, couscous, or polenta. This is a great meal to enjoy some of the summer's bounty of fresh veggies.

1 medium onion, diced

4 garlic cloves, minced

2 Japanese eggplants, cut into 1½-inch pieces

3 zucchini or yellow squash, cut into 1½-inch pieces

1 large orange or yellow bell pepper, diced

4 Roma tomatoes, diced

2 tablespoons tomato paste

2 teaspoons Italian seasoning

¼ to ½ teaspoon red pepper flakes (optional)

Ground black pepper

Salt (optional)

½ cup chopped fresh basil leaves

1. Put the onion, garlic, eggplants, zucchini, bell pepper, tomatoes, tomato paste, Italian seasoning, red pepper flakes (if using), pepper, and salt (if using) in the slow cooker. Stir to combine.

2. Cover and cook on High for 2 to 3 hours or on Low for 4 to 6 hours. Just before serving, stir in the basil.

Per serving: Calories: 144; Fat: 1g; Carbohydrates: 30g; Protein: 6g; Fiber: 9g; Sodium: 22mg

VARIATION TIP: I like to use Japanese eggplants, which are thinner with a softer skin, but you can use one medium eggplant of a more common variety.

Gluten-free, Nut-free, Soy-free

Sweet and Savory Root Veggies and Butternut Squash

SERVES: 4 to 6 | **PREP TIME:** 20 minutes | **COOK TIME:** 3½ to 5 hours on High or 8 to 10 hours on Low

Known as "tzimmes" and pronounced *SEE-miss* or *sim*, depending on which Jewish grandparent you ask, this is a traditional dish served on Jewish holidays representing good fortune and sweet success. There is a bit of peeling and chopping to do, but it's so worth it when you take that first bite. Regular raisins and any combination of prunes, dried cranberries, dried apricots, or dried apples will work here—just be sure to check for added sugar.

1 large sweet potato (about ½ pound), peeled and cut into 1½-inch chunks

2 red or yellow potatoes (about ⅔ pound), unpeeled and cut into 1½-inch chunks

1 medium yam (about ⅓ pound), scrubbed, peeled, and cut into 1½-inch chunks

1 small butternut squash (about 1 pound), peeled and cut into 1½-inch chunks

1 medium onion, diced

4 carrots, cut into 1-inch rounds

2 apples, any variety, peeled and cut into 1-inch chunks

½ cup golden raisins

½ cup pitted dates, quartered

¼ cup maple syrup or Date Syrup (page 134)

Juice from 2 oranges (about 1 cup)

Zest from 1 orange

1 cup Low-Sodium Vegetable Broth (page 136) or store-bought

2 teaspoons ground cinnamon

1 teaspoon ground ginger

1. Put the sweet potato, potatoes, yam, squash, onion, carrots, apples, raisins, dates, syrup, orange juice, orange zest, broth, cinnamon, and ginger in the slow cooker.

2. Cover and cook on High for 3½ to 5 hours or on Low for 8 to 10 hours, until the vegetables are tender.

Per serving: Calories: 460; Fat: 1g; Carbohydrates: 116g; Protein: 7g; Fiber: 15g; Sodium: 92mg

INGREDIENT TIP: Yams have a starchy, mild interior and are closer to a yucca than a sweet potato. You can replace it with a peeled russet potato or another sweet potato.

Mushroom Stroganoff

SERVES: 4 to 6 | **PREP TIME:** 15 minutes | **COOK TIME:** 2 to 3 hours on High or 5 to 6 hours on Low

If I had to choose one dish that has been the most requested from my older daughter since the time she could speak, stroganoff is it. The base is simple enough with mushrooms and onions, but the secret is in the luscious, creamy, slightly tangy sauce. I suggest serving this over noodles like a traditional stroganoff, but it's delicious over rice, mashed potatoes, or baked potatoes. For added creaminess, stir in ½ cup of plant-based sour cream just before serving.

1 large onion, diced

8 ounces white button mushrooms, sliced

8 ounces cremini mushrooms, sliced

2 garlic cloves

1 cup Low-Sodium Vegetable Broth (page 136) or store-bought

½ cup white wine or broth

2 tablespoons tomato paste

3 tablespoons Plant-Based Worcestershire Sauce (page 139) or store-bought

1 teaspoon dried thyme

1 bay leaf

Ground black pepper

Salt (optional)

1½ cups unsweetened plant-based milk, divided

¼ cup whole-wheat flour

¼ cup raw cashews

1 tablespoon nutritional yeast

1 pound cooked whole-grain pasta, for serving

Chopped fresh parsley, for serving (optional)

1. Put the onion, white and cremini mushrooms, garlic, broth, wine, tomato paste, Worcestershire sauce, thyme, bay leaf, pepper, and salt (if using) in the slow cooker. Cover and cook on High for 2 to 3 hours or on Low for 5 to 6 hours.

2. In the last 30 minutes of cooking, whisk together 1 cup of milk and the flour and stir into the slow cooker. Stir occasionally, scraping up any bits from the bottom of the cooker.

3. Meanwhile, add the remaining ½ cup of milk, the cashews, and the nutritional yeast to a blender or food processor and blend until creamy. During the last 10 minutes of cooking, add the mixture to the slow cooker and stir well. Remove and discard the bay leaf. Serve over the cooked pasta and sprinkle with parsley (if using).

Per serving: Calories: 587; Fat: 8g; Carbohydrates: 107g; Protein: 23g; Fiber: 16g; Sodium: 359mg

Nut-free, Soy-free

Portobello Mushroom Fajitas

SERVES: 4 to 6 | **PREP TIME:** 10 minutes | **COOK TIME:** 2 to 3 hours on High or 4 to 5 hours on Low

This is an easy recipe for your next Taco Tuesday. I suggest serving these in tortillas, but it can be tricky to find some if you're omitting salt and oil from your diet. Instead turn this dish into a fajita salad by squeezing the lime juice over your favorite greens and tossing to coat before topping with the mushrooms and your favorite fixings, or serve the dish over rice.

2 large onions, sliced into half-moons

2 medium red bell peppers, sliced into strips

2 medium green bell peppers, sliced into strips

4 portobello mushroom caps, sliced into strips

4 garlic cloves, minced

½ cup Low-Sodium Vegetable Broth (page 136) or store-bought

1 tablespoon chili powder

2 teaspoons ground cumin

1 teaspoon paprika

Ground black pepper

Salt (optional)

Juice of 1 lime

10 to 12 (6-inch) whole-grain flour tortillas, for serving

1 lime, cut into wedges

Salsa, for serving (optional)

Greener Guacamole, (page 145) or store-bought, for serving (optional)

1. Put the onions, red and green bell peppers, mushrooms, garlic, broth, chili powder, cumin, paprika, pepper, and salt (if using) in the slow cooker. Cover and cook on High for 2 to 3 hours or on Low for 4 to 5 hours. Just before serving, stir in the lime juice.

2. When ready to serve, prepare the tortillas. Heat them for a few seconds on each side directly over a gas burner, place in a 350°F oven and bake for 3 minutes, or microwave them for 1 minute or so. Portion the filling into the tortillas, serve with a lime wedge, and top with salsa (if using) and guacamole (if using).

Per serving: Calories: 353; Fat: 7g; Carbohydrates: 62g; Protein: 13g; Fiber: 9g; Sodium: 810mg

VARIATION TIP: Bump up the protein in this dish by draining and rinsing one (15-ounce) can of black or pinto beans and adding it to the pot at the beginning of cooking.

Nut-free

BBQ Pulled Jackfruit Sandwiches

MAKES: 8 sandwiches | **PREP TIME:** 10 minutes | **COOK TIME:** 2 to 3 hours on High or 5 to 6 hours on Low

The first time I heard of pulled jackfruit, I was doubtful. But mixed with BBQ sauce and cooked slowly, this magical fruit does become meaty and pulls like you would want it to. I boost the protein content in these sandwiches by adding a can of navy beans, creating a filling dinner that couldn't be easier—or tastier! I top mine with sauerkraut, pickles, pickled banana peppers, or whatever I'm feeling like that day to add some healthy crunch. This filling also tastes great served over rice.

2 (20-ounce) cans young green jackfruit in water, drained

½ small onion, diced (about ⅓ cup)

1 (14.5-ounce) can navy beans, drained and rinsed

2 cups SOS-Free BBQ Sauce (page 140) or store-bought, plus more for serving

½ cup water

8 whole-grain buns, for serving

1. Put the jackfruit in the slow cooker. Using two forks, pull the pieces apart a bit.

2. Add the onion, beans, BBQ sauce, and water. Stir to combine. Cover and cook on High for 2 to 3 hours or on Low for 5 to 6 hours. Serve in the buns with more BBQ sauce.

Per serving (1 sandwich): Calories: 266; Fat: 3g; Carbohydrates: 53g; Protein: 10g; Fiber: 13g; Sodium: 497mg

INGREDIENT TIP: Jackfruit is a giant, green, scaly fruit the size of a watermelon. You may also find frozen jackfruit, but that is typically ripened and has more of a mango-like flavor and texture. For this recipe, stick to the canned young green jackfruit packed in water. Look for it at your regular grocery store, at an Asian market, or online.

Nut-free, Soy-free

Green Pepper, Potato, and Mushroom Scallopini Sandwiches

MAKES: 6 to 8 sandwiches | **PREP TIME:** 15 minutes | **COOK TIME:** 2 to 3 hours on High or 5 to 6 hours on Low

This dish is one we make when we have out-of-town company arriving "sometime around dinner" and want a casual but delicious meal waiting for them when they arrive. The tomatoes, peppers, potatoes, and mushrooms spooned into a crusty roll takes this to a whole other dimension, but you can also serve this in a bowl for a satisfying gluten-free meal.

1 medium onion, diced

4 garlic cloves, minced

2 medium green bell peppers, cut into 1½-inch pieces

1 pound white button or cremini mushrooms, halved

6 red or yellow potatoes (about 2 pounds), unpeeled and cut into 1½-inch pieces

1 (28-ounce) can no-salt-added crushed tomatoes

⅓ cup red wine or water

1 tablespoon Italian seasoning

¼ teaspoon red pepper flakes (optional)

Ground black pepper

Salt (optional)

10 fresh basil leaves, torn, divided (optional)

6 to 8 (6-inch) whole-grain sub rolls, for serving

1. Put the onion, garlic, bell peppers, mushrooms, potatoes, and tomatoes in the slow cooker. Swirl the red wine inside the empty tomato can and pour everything into the slow cooker. Add the Italian seasoning, red pepper flakes (if using), black pepper, and salt (if using). Stir to combine.

2. Cover and cook on High for 2 to 3 hours or on Low for 5 to 6 hours. Stir occasionally and add more water as needed while cooking to avoid sticking.

3. Before serving, stir in 6 torn basil leaves (if using). Portion about ½ cup of scallopini onto each roll, then top with the remaining 4 torn basil leaves.

Per serving (1 sandwich): Calories: 370; Fat: 2g; Carbohydrates: 70g; Protein: 16g; Fiber: 13g; Sodium: 383mg

VARIATION TIP: This recipe quickly becomes a sausage scallopini by adding a package of plant-based Italian sausage (usually about 4 to 6 sausages, depending on the brand) cut into bite-size pieces to the slow cooker at the beginning of cooking. Top each sandwich with plant-based provolone cheeze or Plant-Based Parmesan (page 137).

Nut-free, Freezable

Lentil Sloppy Joes

MAKES: 8 to 12 sandwiches | **PREP TIME:** 20 minutes | **COOK TIME:** 3 to 4 hours on High or 7 to 8 hours on Low

Sometimes you just want a good hearty sandwich, and this recipe will satisfy your craving. These plant-based sloppy joes are sweet, tangy, chewy, and yes, a little messy, too, which is part of the fun. You could choose to top these with your favorite slaw, pickles, sauerkraut, or raw onions and peppers . . . it's all up to you.

1 cup dried green or brown lentils, rinsed and sorted

1 small onion, finely diced

1 small red or green bell pepper, finely diced

3 garlic cloves, minced

1 (15-ounce) can no-salt-added tomato sauce

2 cups Low-Sodium Vegetable Broth (page 136) or store-bought, divided

2 tablespoons maple syrup or Date Syrup (page 134)

2 tablespoons Plant-Based Worcestershire Sauce (page 139) or store-bought

1 tablespoon tomato paste

2 teaspoons dry mustard

2 teaspoons chili powder

½ teaspoon ground cumin

½ teaspoon smoked paprika

Ground black pepper

Salt (optional)

8 to 12 whole-wheat buns, for serving

1. Put the lentils, onion, bell pepper, garlic, and tomato sauce in the slow cooker. Swirl about ¾ cup of broth in the tomato can and pour it all into the slow cooker.

2. Add the remaining 1¼ cup of broth, the syrup, Worcestershire sauce, tomato paste, mustard, chili powder, cumin, paprika, black pepper, and salt (if using). Cover and cook on High for 3 to 4 hours or on Low for 7 to 8 hours, stirring once per hour to avoid sticking. Serve on the buns.

Per serving (1 sandwich): Calories: 239; Fat: 2g; Carbohydrates: 43g; Protein: 6g; Fiber: 10g; Sodium: 315mg

VARIATION TIP: In place of the lentils and broth, you could use one (12-ounce) package of meatless crumbles or a double recipe of the Shredded Tofu Meaty Crumbles (page 146).

Gluten-free, Nut-free, Soy-free

Black Bean, Corn, and Salsa Fiesta

SERVES: 4 to 6 | **PREP TIME:** 10 minutes | **COOK TIME:** 2 to 3 hours on High or 5 to 6 hours on Low

This Southwestern-inspired dish has been a family favorite for many years. Whether I make the rice separately or at the same time, I love my bowl with some fresh Greener Guacamole (page 145) dolloped on top. Add even more protein by incorporating a package of frozen grilled plant-based chick'n strips at the beginning of the cooking time.

2 (14.5-ounce) cans black beans, drained and rinsed

4 cups frozen corn

2 cups salsa

2 teaspoons chili powder

1 teaspoon ground cumin

1 teaspoon garlic powder

Ground black pepper

Salt (optional)

⅔ cup Cheeze Sauce (pages 141–143) or store-bought cheeze sauce

3 cups cooked brown rice, for serving

1 lime, cut into wedges, for serving (optional)

½ small bunch cilantro, chopped, for serving (optional)

1. Put the beans, corn, salsa, chili powder, cumin, garlic powder, pepper, and salt (if using) in the slow cooker. Stir to combine. Cover and cook on High for 2 to 3 hours or on Low for 5 to 6 hours.

2. During the last 10 minutes of cooking, gently stir in the cheeze sauce. Portion the cooked rice into bowls and top with the black bean, corn, and salsa fiesta. Serve each bowl with a lime wedge (if using) and a sprinkle of cilantro (if using).

Per serving: Calories: 604; Fat: 6g; Carbohydrates: 121g; Protein: 25g; Fiber: 25g; Sodium: 1,006mg

COOKING TIP: On my busiest days, I'll add 1½ cups of uncooked brown rice and 3 cups of broth to step 1, letting everything cook together. The end result is a bit more like a casserole than a hearty sauce over rice.

INGREDIENT TIP: When choosing your salsa, read labels carefully if you're omitting salt or sugar from your diet. You can also replace the salsa with one (15-ounce) can diced tomatoes; ½ onion, diced; 2 minced garlic cloves; and one (4-ounce) can diced green chiles.

Gluten-free, Nut-free, Soy-free

Southwestern Quinoa Taco Bowls

SERVES: 4 to 6 | **PREP TIME:** 15 minutes | **COOK TIME:** 2 to 3 hours on High
or 4 to 6 hours on Low

With so many ways to make taco filling, you could enjoy a different kind of taco every day of the week. This recipe for a taco bowl features quinoa, a grain that originated with the Incas in the mountains of South America, along with other traditional South American flavors like corn and a healthy dose of chili powder.

1 medium onion, diced

1 medium green or red bell pepper, diced

4 garlic cloves, minced

2 (14.5-ounce) can black beans

1½ cups frozen corn

1½ cups quinoa, rinsed

2¼ cups Low-Sodium Vegetable Broth (page 136) or store-bought

1 (8-ounce) can tomato sauce

2 tablespoons chili powder

1 teaspoon ground cumin

1 teaspoon paprika

Ground black pepper

Salt (optional)

½ bunch cilantro, chopped

1 head shredded lettuce of choice, for serving

1 (8-ounce) container grape tomatoes, for serving

Greener Guacamole (page 145) or store-bought, for serving (optional)

1 lime, sliced into wedges, for serving

1. Put the onion, bell pepper, garlic, beans, corn, quinoa, broth, tomato sauce, chili powder, cumin, paprika, pepper, and salt (if using) in the slow cooker. Stir to combine. Cover and cook on High for 2 to 3 hours or on Low for 4 to 6 hours. Just before serving, mix in the cilantro.

2. Divide the lettuce among bowls and top each with about 1 cup of filling, a handful of tomatoes, and a dollop of guacamole (if using). Serve with a lime wedge.

Per serving: Calories: 591; Fat: 7g; Carbohydrates: 112g; Protein: 28g; Fiber: 30g; Sodium: 440mg

VARIATION TIP: Instead of a bowl, choose your favorite type of tortilla and make tacos. Add some plant-based sour cream and shredded cheeze or a dollop of homemade Cheeze Sauce (pages 141–143).

Nut-free

Hawaiian-Inspired Pepper Pot with Brown Rice

SERVES: 4 to 6 | **PREP TIME:** 15 minutes | **COOK TIME:** 2 to 3 hours on High or 5 to 6 hours on Low

My husband and I spent our honeymoon in Hawaii, and we fell in love with the flavors of the islands. In this dish, reminiscent of classic Hawaiian tastes, fresh veggies mix with pineapple and cook together with rice in a sweet garlic, ginger, and soy sauce mixture. Be careful when you bite into the pineapple: the juice locked inside is hot!

Nonstick cooking spray (optional)

1 medium onion, diced

1 medium red bell pepper, diced

1 medium green bell pepper, diced

1½ cups brown rice

3 cups Low-Sodium Vegetable Broth (page 136) or store-bought

1 (20-ounce) can pineapple pieces in juice, undrained

2 tablespoons low-sodium soy sauce, tamari, or coconut aminos

2 tablespoons Date Syrup (page 134) or maple syrup

1 piece (1-inch) fresh ginger, peeled and minced, or 1 teaspoon ground ginger

1 teaspoon garlic powder

Ground black pepper

Salt (optional)

1. Coat the inside of the slow cooker with cooking spray (if using) or line it with a slow cooker liner.

2. Add the onion, red and green bell peppers, rice, broth, pineapple, soy sauce, syrup, ginger, garlic powder, black pepper, and salt (if using). Stir well to combine.

3. Cover and cook on High for 2 to 3 hours or on Low for 5 to 6 hours. Stir occasionally during the last hour of cooking to keep the rice from settling and overcooking.

Per serving: Calories: 379; Fat: 3g; Carbohydrates: 87g; Protein: 9g; Fiber: 7g; Sodium: 309mg

VARIATION TIP: This recipe is reminiscent of a pepper steak, so you could add a package of grilled beef-like strips, such as Quorn brand, at the beginning of the cooking time. Alternatively, cook the rice separately and omit the 3 cups of broth from the recipe.

Gluten-free, Nut-free, Soy-free

Cajun-Style Jambalaya

SERVES: 4 to 6 | **PREP TIME:** 15 minutes | **COOK TIME:** 3 to 4 hours on High or 7 to 8 hours on Low

Each year on Mardi Gras, I make a Cajun-inspired dish like jambalaya to celebrate. This filling recipe packs a bit of heat thanks to the cayenne. You can add more or leave it out completely to your preference. Some plant-based andouille sausage and plant-based chick'n would also be great to try together in this dish.

Nonstick cooking spray (optional)

1 medium onion, diced

1 medium green bell pepper, diced

3 celery stalks, diced

4 garlic cloves, minced

1 (14.5-ounce) can no-salt-added diced tomatoes

1 (14.5-ounce) can kidney beans, drained and rinsed

1 bay leaf

2 cups uncooked brown rice

1 (8-ounce) can tomato sauce

4 cups Low-Sodium Vegetable Broth (page 136) or store-bought

1 teaspoon dried thyme

1 teaspoon dried oregano

2 teaspoons paprika

½ teaspoon cayenne powder

Ground black pepper

Salt (optional)

1. Coat the inside of the slow cooker with cooking spray (if using) or line it with a slow cooker liner.

2. Add the onion, bell pepper, celery, garlic, tomatoes, beans, bay leaf, rice, tomato sauce, broth, thyme, oregano, paprika, cayenne, black pepper, and salt (if using).

3. Cover and cook on High for 3 to 4 hours or on Low for 7 to 8 hours, stirring once per hour after the first two hours to avoid sticking. Remove and discard the bay leaf before serving.

Per serving: Calories: 466; Fat: 4g; Carbohydrates: 102g; Protein: 15g; Fiber: 15g; Sodium: 489mg

Nut-free, Soy-free

Garlic Lovers' Chili Mac and Cheeze

SERVES: 4 to 6 | **PREP TIME:** 15 minutes | **COOK TIME:** 2 to 3 hours on High or 4 to 6 hours on Low

In my house whenever I had leftover chili, the next day it would often become chili mac. My family loved it so much that I decided to make a whole pot of it on purpose. This version is loaded with garlic, but you can always use less depending on your preference.

12 garlic cloves, sliced

1 medium onion, diced

2 medium green or red bell peppers, diced

1 (14.5-ounce) can kidney beans, drained and rinsed

1 (28-ounce) can no-salt-added diced tomatoes

1 tablespoon chili powder

2 teaspoons cocoa powder

2 teaspoons ground cumin

2 teaspoons garlic powder

2 teaspoons paprika

1 teaspoon dried oregano

Ground black pepper

Salt (optional)

4 cups Low-Sodium Vegetable Broth (page 136) or store-bought

1 pound macaroni pasta, uncooked

2 cups Cheeze Sauce (pages 141–143) or store-bought cheeze sauce

1. Put the garlic, onion, bell peppers, beans, tomatoes, chili powder, cocoa powder, cumin, garlic powder, paprika, oregano, black pepper, salt (if using), and broth in the slow cooker. Stir to combine. Cover and cook on High for 2 to 3 hours or on Low for 4 to 6 hours.

2. In the last 30 minutes of cooking, add the pasta to the slow cooker and stir well to combine. Stir it every 10 minutes and check for your preferred doneness. Before serving, stir in the cheeze sauce and mix well.

Per serving: Calories: 738; Fat: 9g; Carbohydrates: 137g; Protein: 31g; Fiber: 18g; Sodium: 301mg

Spinach Lasagna

SERVES: 4 to 6 | **PREP TIME:** 20 minutes | **COOK TIME:** 4 to 5 hours on Low, plus 1 hour to set

After my older daughter's first semester away at college, she requested this lasagna for her homecoming meal. Growing up with my Italian roots, I'll admit I was skeptical about a lasagna made with tofu standing in for ricotta cheese, but I was pleasantly surprised. Do your best to break the lasagna noodles to fit into your slow cooker. There's no need to precook them. They hydrate beautifully as they cook, creating a lasagna even my grandmother would be proud of.

¼ cup unsweetened plant-based milk

1 (14-ounce) package silken tofu

1 (14-ounce) package firm tofu, drained

Juice from 1 lemon (about ¼ cup)

¼ cup nutritional yeast

2 teaspoons garlic powder

2 teaspoons Italian seasoning

Ground black pepper

Salt (optional)

7 to 8 cups Mama Mia Marinara Sauce (page 150) or store-bought, divided

1 package whole-grain lasagna noodles, divided

2 (10-ounce) packages frozen spinach, thawed and squeezed dry, divided

½ cup Plant-Based Parmesan (page 137) or store-bought, divided (optional)

1. In a blender or food processor, combine the milk, silken tofu, firm tofu, lemon juice, nutritional yeast, garlic powder, Italian seasoning, pepper, and salt (if using). Blend well.

2. Put about 1½ cups of marinara sauce in the slow cooker, coating the bottom well. Place 3 to 6 lasagna noodles over the sauce, breaking them into pieces so they fit without overlapping. Top with a third of the tofu mixture. Cover that layer with a third of the spinach. Repeat the process until all of the ingredients have been used, making sure all the noodles are well covered in sauce. Top with ¼ cup of parmesan (if using).

3. Cover and cook on Low for 4 to 5 hours. After the cooking time ends, turn off the slow cooker. The lasagna will set as it cools. Keep the lid on and allow it to set for at least 15 minutes or up to 1 hour. Serve with the remaining ¼ cup of parmesan (if using).

Per serving: Calories: 681; Fat: 12g; Carbohydrates: 105g; Protein: 38g; Fiber: 18g; Sodium: 69mg

CHAPTER SEVEN

Desserts

Creamy Dreamy
Brown Rice Pudding
120

Gooey Bittersweet
Chocolate Pudding Cake
124

Pumpkin Pie
Oatmeal Parfaits
121

Poppy's
Carrot Cake
126

Chocolate's Best
Friends Brownies
122

"Here Comes
Autumn" Apple Crisp
128

Peach
Cobbler
123

Lemon
Poppy Seed Cake
130

Gluten-free, Nut-free, Soy-free

Creamy Dreamy Brown Rice Pudding

SERVES: 6 to 8 | **PREP TIME:** 5 minutes | **COOK TIME:** 2 to 3 hours on High or 3 to 4 hours on Low

Many cultures around the world have some version of rice pudding cooked simply with rice and milk or cream with flavoring. Of course, this version uses fully plant-based, whole-food ingredients to make a delicious, creamy treat that is ideal for dessert made simply in the slow cooker. You can serve this warm or chill it in the refrigerator before serving. Try it both ways and see which is your favorite!

Nonstick cooking spray (optional)

1 cup brown rice

4 cups unsweetened vanilla plant-based milk

¼ cup maple syrup or Date Syrup (page 134)

2 teaspoons ground cinnamon

2 teaspoons vanilla extract

½ cup raisins, for topping (optional)

1. Coat the inside of the slow cooker with cooking spray (if using) or line it with a slow cooker liner.

2. Add the rice, milk, syrup, cinnamon, and vanilla, and stir to combine.

3. Cover and cook on High for 2 to 3 hours or on Low for 3 to 4 hours, stirring when there is an hour left to check for doneness and your preference for the rice. Cook it longer for creamier pudding or shorter for a more toothsome texture. Just before serving, top with the raisins (if using) for extra sweetness and texture.

Per serving: Calories: 157; Fat: 3g; Carbohydrates: 34g; Protein: 3g; Fiber: 3g; Sodium: 115mg

VARIATION TIP: Add walnuts for another layer of texture or try dried apricots instead of raisins and add shelled pistachios for a Middle Eastern–influenced flavor. If serving cold, try fresh berries and lime zest. For adults only, soak the raisins in 1 to 2 tablespoons of rum for about 20 minutes before topping the pudding.

Gluten-free, Soy-free

Pumpkin Pie Oatmeal Parfaits

MAKES: 6 parfaits | **PREP TIME:** 20 minutes | **COOK TIME:** 7 hours on Low

The contrasts in this recipe make it a winner: warm and chewy pumpkin pie–flavored oats, crunchy pecans, cool whipped coconut cream, and sweet maple syrup. Note that pumpkin puree is used, not pumpkin pie filling.

Nonstick cooking spray (optional)

1 (15-ounce) can coconut cream

2 cups steel-cut oats

4 cups water

1 (15-ounce) can pumpkin puree

2 teaspoons ground cinnamon, divided

1 teaspoon ground nutmeg, divided

½ teaspoon ground cloves

½ teaspoon ground ginger

½ cup maple syrup, plus 3 to 4 tablespoons more for serving

1½ cups rolled oats

¾ cup chopped pecans (optional)

1. Coat the inside of the slow cooker with cooking spray (if using) or line it with a slow cooker liner. Place the unopened can of coconut cream into the refrigerator to chill.

2. Add the steel-cut oats, water, pumpkin puree, 1 teaspoon of cinnamon, ½ teaspoon of nutmeg, the cloves, ginger, and maple syrup. Stir to combine. Cover and cook on Low for 7 hours. After cooking, stir well.

3. While the steel-cut oats cook, preheat the oven to 350°F. On a parchment-lined baking sheet, spread out the rolled oats and pecans (if using) in a single layer and sprinkle with the remaining 1 teaspoon of cinnamon and ½ teaspoon of nutmeg. Bake for 10 minutes. Set the crumble aside to cool and store loosely covered at room temperature until the steel-cut oats are done cooking.

4. Just before serving, pour the cold coconut cream into a medium bowl. Using an electric beater, whip the cream for about 1 minute, until it becomes thick.

5. For each parfait, layer 3 tablespoons of the crumble, about ½ teaspoon of the maple syrup, 2 to 3 tablespoons of the warm pumpkin oatmeal, and about 2 tablespoons of the whipped cream. Continue layering in this order until your glass is full, finishing with the whipped cream on top, a sprinkle of the crumble, and a tiny drizzle more of maple syrup.

Per serving (1 parfait): Calories: 497; Fat: 18g; Carbohydrates: 76g; Protein: 11g; Fiber: 10g; Sodium: 31mg

Gluten-free, Nut-free, Soy-free

Chocolate's Best Friends Brownies

MAKES: about 2 dozen brownies | **PREP TIME:** 15 minutes
COOK TIME: 3½ hours on Low, plus 1 hour to cool

Chocolate has three best friends that intensify its flavor—vanilla, cinnamon, and coffee—and you'll find all of them in this recipe. White beans give these brownies their dense, moist texture and up the fiber without adding any "beany" flavor.

1¼ cups oats

¾ cup white beans, drained, and rinsed

¾ cup plus 3 tablespoons maple syrup

¼ cup plus 2 tablespoons unsweetened applesauce

1½ teaspoons vanilla extract

1½ teaspoons baking powder

½ teaspoon salt (optional)

¾ cup unsweetened cocoa powder

½ teaspoon ground cinnamon

1 teaspoon instant coffee

1. Crumple two pieces of aluminum foil to form a ring around the interior base of the slow cooker. Add a liner or piece of parchment and set the slow cooker to Low to preheat.

2. Put the oats in a blender or food processor and process into oat flour. Pour it into a small bowl and set aside.

3. Add the beans, maple syrup, applesauce, and vanilla to the blender and blend until well combined, about 1 minute. Add the oat flour, baking powder, salt (if using), cocoa powder, cinnamon, and instant coffee. Blend until smooth and thick, scraping down the sides as needed.

4. Spread the batter into the prepared slow cooker. Cover and cook on Low for 3½ hours. Turn off the slow cooker, remove the cover, and let the brownies cool completely before slicing, at least 1 hour. Store at room temperature for 2 to 3 days.

Per serving (1 brownie): Calories: 63; Fat: 1g; Carbohydrates: 14g; Protein: 2g; Fiber: 2g; Sodium: 35mg

Gluten-free, Nut-free, Soy-free

Peach Cobbler

SERVES: 6 to 8 | **PREP TIME:** 15 minutes | **COOK TIME:** 1 to 2 hours on High or 2 to 3 hours on Low

Enjoying fruit for dessert is a fabulous way to end a meal on a whole-food plant-based diet. Turning that fruit into a cobbler makes it extra special. This recipe uses canned peaches because they are available year-round. Be sure to get those that come in juice and not heavy syrup. You'll use a bit of that juice to sweeten the cobbler.

FOR THE FILLING

2 (15-ounce) cans peaches in juice

½ teaspoon ground cinnamon

½ teaspoon ground ginger

3 tablespoons maple syrup or Date Syrup (page 134)

2 tablespoons cornstarch

FOR THE TOPPING

1 cup rolled oats

¼ teaspoon ground cinnamon

2 tablespoons coconut cream

1 tablespoon liquid from the canned peaches

4 tablespoons Date Syrup (page 134)

1. Make the filling: Remove the peaches from the cans, reserving the juice. Slice the peaches into bite-size chunks and put them in the slow cooker. Stir in the cinnamon, ginger, syrup, and cornstarch.

2. Make the topping and cook: In a medium bowl, combine the oats, cinnamon, coconut cream, canned peach liquid, and date syrup. Stir together until the oats are wet and crumbly. Sprinkle over the peaches in the slow cooker.

3. To keep the condensation that forms on the inside of the lid away from the topping, stretch a clean dish towel or several layers of paper towels over the top of the slow cooker, but not touching the food, and place the lid on top of the towel(s). If you skip this step, you will have a soggy result. Cook on High for 1 to 2 hours or on Low for 2 to 3 hours.

Per serving: Calories: 196; Fat: 2g; Carbohydrates: 44g; Protein: 3g; Fiber: 4g; Sodium: 16mg

VARIATION TIP: For a sweeter, more traditional cobbler topping, substitute 2 tablespoons of plant-based butter for the coconut cream and ½ cup of brown sugar for the date syrup and omit the liquid from the canned peaches.

Nut-free, Soy-free

Gooey Bittersweet Chocolate Pudding Cake

SERVES: 6 to 8 | **PREP TIME:** 15 minutes | **COOK TIME:** 3 to 4 hours on Low

This informal, old-fashioned dessert goes back to at least the 1800s. Simultaneously both a cake and a pudding, the slightly bittersweet treat is amped up with a bit of instant coffee (I use decaf so I can enjoy this after dinner and still sleep!), vanilla, and cinnamon.

FOR THE CAKE

1 cup whole-wheat flour

¼ cup cocoa powder

2 teaspoons baking powder

½ teaspoon ground cinnamon

¼ teaspoon salt (optional)

⅓ cup unsweetened applesauce

2 teaspoons vanilla extract

⅔ cup unsweetened vanilla or plain plant-based milk

2 tablespoons Date Syrup (page 134) or maple syrup

Nonstick cooking spray (optional)

FOR THE PUDDING

¼ cup cocoa powder

1 teaspoon instant coffee

½ cup Date Syrup (page 134) or maple syrup

1 teaspoon vanilla extract

1 cup hot water

1. Make the cake: In a medium bowl, whisk together the flour, cocoa powder, baking powder, cinnamon, and salt (if using).

2. In a separate medium bowl, whisk together the applesauce, vanilla, milk, and date syrup. Pour the applesauce mixture into the flour mixture and stir until just fully combined. Do not overmix.

3. Coat the inside of the slow cooker with cooking spray (if using) or line it with a slow cooker liner. Add the cake batter and spread it over the bottom of the slow cooker.

4. Make the pudding: In a medium bowl, whisk together the cocoa powder, coffee, date syrup, vanilla, and hot water. Pour over the cake ingredients in the slow cooker. The mixture will be watery.

5. Cover and cook on Low for 3 to 4 hours. When it is ready to serve, the cake will look dry on top and will have achieved a pudding-like texture below the surface. Enjoy it immediately for best results.

Per serving: Calories: 195; Fat: 2g; Carbohydrates: 44g; Protein: 4g; Fiber: 4g; Sodium: 201mg

INGREDIENT TIP: Don't be tempted to use coffee grounds or brewed coffee in this recipe. The instant coffee granules provide the ideal flavor and texture for the cake. If you want to avoid buying a lot, look for a small box with premeasured packets. You can also use it in Chocolate's Best Friends Brownies on page 122.

Gluten-free, Soy-free

Poppy's Carrot Cake

SERVES: 6 to 8 | **PREP TIME:** 20 minutes | **COOK TIME:** 3 hours on Low, plus 30 minutes to cool

My dad's favorite dessert was carrot cake. This version, naturally sweetened with bananas, date syrup, and raisins, is a showstopper, coming out moist and delicious every time. I love the extra body and texture provided by keeping some of the oats whole. Enjoy this cake frosted or unfrosted—and if you have it for breakfast, I won't tell.

**FOR THE
CARROT CAKE**

Nonstick cooking spray (optional)

1 tablespoon ground flaxseed

2½ tablespoons water

2¼ cups rolled oats, divided

1¾ teaspoons ground cinnamon

¾ teaspoon ground nutmeg

¾ teaspoon ground ginger

2 teaspoons baking powder

1 teaspoon baking soda

1 cup unsweetened plant-based milk

¾ cup raisins, divided

¼ cup unsweetened applesauce

⅓ cup Date Syrup (page 134) or maple syrup

1 medium banana, peeled and broken into pieces

1 teaspoon vanilla extract

2 cups grated carrots

½ cup walnut pieces (optional)

FOR THE FROSTING

¾ cup raw cashews

6 pitted Medjool dates, chopped

½ teaspoon ground ginger

⅓ to ½ cup water

2 tablespoons coconut cream

1. Prepare the slow cooker by folding two long sheets of aluminum foil and placing them perpendicular to each other (crisscross) in the bottom of the slow cooker to create "handles" that will come out over the top of the slow cooker. Coat the inside of the slow cooker and foil with cooking spray (if using) or line it with a slow cooker liner.

2. Make the carrot cake: Make a flax egg in a small bowl by mixing together the flaxseed and the water. Set aside.

3. In a blender or food processor, combine 1¾ cups of oats, the cinnamon, nutmeg, ginger, baking powder, and baking soda. Blend until the oats are turned into a flour. Pour into a large bowl and set aside. Add the remaining ½ cup of whole oats to the dry ingredients.

4. Without rinsing the blender or food processor, add the milk, ¼ cup of raisins, apple-sauce, syrup, banana, vanilla, and the flax egg. Process until smooth and the raisins are broken down. Pour over the dry ingredients. Add the carrots, the remaining ½ cup of raisins, and the walnuts (if using), and stir well to combine.

5. Pour the mixture into the prepared slow cooker. Stretch a clean dish towel or a few layers of paper towels over the top of the slow cooker and cover. Cook on Low for 3 hours. The carrot cake is ready when a toothpick inserted in the center comes out clean. Remove the insert from the slow cooker and cool on a wire rack for at least 30 minutes before removing the cake from the insert. Allow to cool completely before frosting.

6. Make the frosting: Put the cashews, dates, and ginger in a blender or food proces-sor. Cover with just enough water to submerge the cashews and dates. Let the mixture soak for up to 1 hour to soften. Add the coconut cream and blend well until creamy. The frosting will thicken slightly as it sits.

Per serving: Calories: 436; Fat: 11g; Carbohydrates: 81g; Protein: 9g; Fiber: 9g; Sodium: 447mg

Gluten-Free, Soy-Free

"Here Comes Autumn" Apple Crisp

SERVES: 4 to 6 | **PREP TIME:** 15 minutes | **COOK TIME:** 2 to 3 hours on High or 4 to 5 hours on Low

When my girls were little, I'd take my family apple picking in the country in autumn. The heavenly scent of apples baking with cinnamon instantly brings me back to those days. This sweet treat has a crunchy texture from the topping and melt-in-your-mouth goodness of the baked apples and warm spices. Plus, you don't have to peel the apples!

FOR THE APPLE BASE

- 6 apples (about 2 pounds), any variety, cored and thinly sliced
- 1 tablespoon lemon juice
- 2 tablespoons maple syrup
- 1 teaspoon ground cinnamon
- ½ teaspoon grated nutmeg

FOR THE TOPPING

- ¾ cup chopped pecans
- ½ cup almond meal or almond flour
- ½ cup rolled oats
- 3 tablespoons maple syrup
- ½ teaspoon ground cinnamon
- ¼ teaspoon grated nutmeg

1. Make the apple base: Put the apples in the slow cooker and sprinkle with the lemon juice, tossing well to coat the apples completely. Stir in the maple syrup, cinnamon, and nutmeg until the syrup and spices cover every apple slice. Spread the apples out in an even layer.

2. Make the topping and cook: In a medium bowl, combine the pecans, almond meal or flour, oats, maple syrup, cinnamon, and nutmeg. Mix well until crumbles form. Spoon the mixture evenly over the apples.

3. To keep the condensation that forms on the inside of the lid away from the topping, stretch a clean dish towel or several layers of paper towels across the top of the slow cooker, but not touching the food, and place the lid on top of the towel(s). If you skip this step, you will have a soggy result rather than a crunchy crumble.

4. Cook on High for 2 to 3 hours or on Low for 4 to 5 hours, until the apples are soft and cooked through.

Per serving: Calories: 469; Fat: 23g; Carbohydrates: 68g; Protein: 7g; Fiber: 12g; Sodium: 11mg

VARIATION TIP: You can top this crisp with whipped coconut cream (see step 4 on page 121) or plant-based ice cream. You can make your own plant-based ice cream by peeling and freezing two bananas and blending them with a little plant-based milk.

Nut-free, Soy-free

Lemon Poppy Seed Cake

SERVES: 6 to 8 | **PREP TIME:** 15 minutes | **COOK TIME:** 2 to 2½ hours on High, plus 30 minutes to cool

When you feel like having something bright and sunny, give this tangy lemon cake a try. The flavor of both the lemon zest and lemon juice shines through, and a pinch of turmeric makes the color pop (and adds a bit of extra antioxidant power).

FOR THE CAKE

Nonstick cooking spray (optional)

1 cup rolled oats, blended into flour

1 cup white whole-wheat flour

1 teaspoon baking powder

½ teaspoon baking soda

¼ teaspoon ground turmeric

⅓ cup maple syrup

½ cup unsweetened plant-based milk

Zest of 1 lemon (about 1 tablespoon)

⅓ cup lemon juice

3 tablespoons aquafaba (see page 10)

1½ teaspoons apple cider vinegar

1½ teaspoons poppy seeds

FOR THE GLAZE

3 tablespoons unsweetened shredded coconut

3 tablespoons unsweetened plant-based milk

2 tablespoons maple syrup or Date Syrup (page 134)

1 teaspoon lemon zest

Juice from ½ lemon (about 2 teaspoons)

1. Prepare the slow cooker by folding two long sheets of aluminum foil and placing them perpendicular to each other (crisscross) in the bottom of the slow cooker to create "handles" that will come out over the top of the slow cooker. Coat the inside of the slow cooker and the foil with cooking spray (if using) or line it with a slow cooker liner.

2. Make the cake: In a large bowl, whisk together the the oat flour, whole-wheat flour, baking powder, baking soda, and turmeric. Set aside.

3. In a medium bowl, whisk together the maple syrup, milk, lemon zest, lemon juice, aquafaba, and vinegar. Stir in the poppy seeds. Pour the milk mixture into the flour mixture and stir well with a wooden spoon. You will notice a little foaming. That is the acid from the lemons and vinegar reacting with the baking powder and is what will give the cake a nice lift and tang.

4. To keep the condensation that forms on the inside of the lid away from the cake as it bakes, stretch a clean dish towel or several layers of paper towels across the top of the slow cooker, but not touching the food, and place the lid on top of the towel(s). If you skip this step, you will have a soggy result.

5. Cook on High for 2 to 2½ hours. To test for doneness, insert a toothpick into the center of the cake; when it comes out clean, the cake is done. Remove the interior bowl from the slow cooker and allow the cake to cool for at least 30 minutes before removing the cake from the liner.

6. Make the glaze: When the cake is cool, put the coconut in a food processor or blender and process until smooth, scraping down the sides as needed. Add the milk, syrup, lemon zest, and lemon juice and blend until smooth. Pour over the cake and serve immediately.

Per serving: Calories: 212; Fat: 4g; Carbohydrates: 43g; Protein: 5g; Fiber: 4g; Sodium: 107mg

CHAPTER EIGHT

Basics and Bonus Recipes

Date Syrup
134

Chili Powder
135

Low-Sodium
Vegetable Broth
136

Plant-Based
Parmesan
137

Plant-Based
Fish Sauce
138

Plant-Based
Worcestershire Sauce
139

SOS-Free
BBQ Sauce
140

20-Minute Cashew
Cheeze Sauce
141

10-Minute White
Bean Cheeze Sauce
142

5-Minute Tofu
Cheeze Sauce
143

Oil-Free
Hummus
144

Greener
Guacamole
145

Shredded Tofu
Meaty Crumbles
146

Chipotle Peppers
in Adobo Sauce
148

Mama Mia
Marinara Sauce
150

Gluten-free, Nut-free, Soy-free

Date Syrup

MAKES: 1½ to 2 cups | **PREP TIME:** 2 hours 20 minutes | **COOK TIME:** 1 hour

This sweetener has only two ingredients and is a great substitute for sugar or maple syrup in recipes like Strawberries and Cream Overnight Oatmeal (page 21) and Creamy Dreamy Brown Rice Pudding (page 120). While it has several steps—soaking, simmering, straining, and reducing—it'll keep in the refrigerator for up to 3 weeks. Keep in mind that it's sweeter than traditional sugars, so you'll want to use half the amount of date syrup if you're using it to replace sugar in other recipes.

1 pound pitted dates,
coarsely chopped

4 cups water, plus more
for soaking

1. Place the dates in a large bowl and cover with water. Soak for 20 minutes to remove any impurities. Drain and rinse.

2. In a medium saucepan, combine the dates and 4 cups of water. Cover and bring to a boil over high heat. Turn the heat to low and simmer, covered, for at least 1 hour and up to 2 hours—the longer the better.

3. Allow the mixture to cool. Strain the dates through a clean dish towel or several layers of cheesecloth placed over a large bowl to reserve the liquid. Wring the cloth around the date pulp to squeeze out all the liquid. Discard the dried pulp.

4. Return the liquid to the saucepan and bring to a boil uncovered. Cook for 45 to 60 minutes, stirring occasionally, until reduced to less than half and the syrup coats the back of a wooden spoon. The longer you reduce it, the thicker the syrup will become, and it will continue to thicken as it cools. I stop reducing when there are about 1½ cups or so of syrup. Pour into a glass container with a tight-fitting lid and store in the refrigerator.

Per serving (1 tablespoon): Calories: 53; Fat: <1g; Carbohydrates: 14g; Protein: 1g; Fiber: 2g; Sodium: <1mg

Gluten-free, Nut-free, Soy-free

Chili Powder

MAKES: about ½ cup | **PREP TIME:** 15 minutes

I love experimenting with blends of dried chiles when I make my own chili powder, which I do about once a month. I use it in recipes like Mama's Mighty Meatless Award-Winning Chili (page 90) and Southwestern Quinoa Taco Bowls (page 112), and I find that store-bought versions can't beat the fresh, smoky, slightly spicy flavor of homemade.

3 arbol chiles

5 guajillo chiles

5 California chiles

2 tablespoons cumin seeds (not ground)

2 tablespoons garlic powder

1 tablespoon dried oregano

1 tablespoon onion powder

1. Heat a cast-iron skillet over high heat. As the skillet heats up, remove and discard the stems and seeds from the arbol, guajillo, and California chiles.

2. Place the chiles in the hot, dry skillet and roast for 3 to 5 minutes, turning occasionally, until the color slightly changes and the chiles become softer. Transfer the chiles to a blender or food processor.

3. Put the cumin seeds in the hot skillet and toast until they begin popping. Immediately transfer them to the blender, along with the garlic powder, oregano, and onion powder.

4. Cover tightly and blend into a fine powder. Allow the powder to settle for 2 to 3 minutes before removing the lid. Store in a cool, dry location for up to 6 months.

Per serving (1 teaspoon): Calories: 7; Fat: <1g; Carbohydrates: 1g; Protein: <1g; Fiber: <1g; Sodium: 2mg

COOKING TIP: To roast the chiles and cumin seeds in the oven, preheat the oven to 350°F and place the chiles in a single layer on a baking sheet. Roast for 4 to 7 minutes, until they are slightly puffed and toasted, being careful not to burn them. After cooling enough to handle, remove the stems and seeds and proceed with the recipe.

VARIATION TIP: Swap out the types of dried chiles to determine your favorite blend. Arbol chiles are a standard and have a bit of heat. Beyond those, try cascabel, New Mexico, pasilla, chipotle, and Colorado chiles, and whatever other varieties you can find.

Gluten-free, Nut-free, Soy-free, Freezable

Low-Sodium Vegetable Broth

MAKES: about 3 quarts | **PREP TIME:** 5 minutes | **COOK TIME:** 3 hours

My go-to method for veggie broth is to save all my scraps from prepping raw veggies for recipes—potato and carrot peels, onion skins and ends, leaves and ends from celery, broccoli stems, bell pepper stems and seeds, and so forth. I keep these in my freezer in a bag and add to it each time I cook. When the bag is full, I make vegetable broth by covering it all with water and letting it boil for a few hours. This cookbook will definitely get you to fill up your veggie bag quickly, but in case you don't have a freezer full of scraps on hand, here's how to get vegetable broth right now.

4 carrots, chopped

2 medium onions, skins included, quartered

4 celery stalks, chopped

6 garlic cloves, unpeeled and crushed

2 to 3 kale leaves and stems, chopped

1 sprig fresh rosemary

3 to 5 springs fresh thyme

1 bunch parsley stems

2 bay leaves

2 to 4 black peppercorns

3 quarts water

1. Place a large stock pot over high heat and toss in the carrots, onions, and celery. Dry sauté for 5 minutes, adding a tablespoon or so of water as needed to keep them from sticking.

2. Add the garlic, kale, rosemary, thyme, parsley stems, bay leaves, and peppercorns and stir. Add the water.

3. Cover, bring to a boil, and then lower the heat. Simmer for 2 to 3 hours. Strain the broth and freeze for up to 6 months.

Per serving (1 cup): Calories: 11; Fat: <1g; Carbohydrates: 3g; Protein: <1g; Fiber: 1g; Sodium: 15mg

INGREDIENT TIP: Most recipes use the leaves of parsley but discard the woody stems. Here the stems add nice flavor to our veggie broth before making their way to the compost bin. Save the leaves for other recipes like the Savory Slow Cooker Stuffing (page 49) or as a garnish for Mushroom Stroganoff (page 104).

Gluten-free, Soy-free

Plant-Based Parmesan

MAKES: 1 heaping cup | **PREP TIME:** 5 minutes

Sometimes a sprinkle of something cheesy is all you need to finish a dish and bring it to the next level. Use this plant-based parmesan to top the Spinach Lasagna (page 116); Hearty Potato, Tomato, and Green Beans Stufato (page 80); Green Pepper, Potato, and Mushroom Scallopini Sandwiches (page 108); and any other salads or sandwiches. You'll be pleasantly surprised how easy it is to re-create the flavor and texture of traditional cheese.

1 cup raw cashews

⅓ cup nutritional yeast

¾ teaspoon garlic powder

½ teaspoon salt (optional)

1. In a blender or food processor, combine the cashews, nutritional yeast, garlic powder, and salt (if using).

2. Blend on medium-high until the mixture has the texture of grated parmesan cheese. You may need to stop and start the blender or food processor a couple of times to make sure the nuts are not clumping together on the bottom. Store in a glass or plastic container in the refrigerator for up to 1 month.

Per serving (¼ cup): Calories: 219; Fat: 15g; Carbohydrates: 14g; Protein: 11g; Fiber: 4g; Sodium: 8mg

Nut-free

Plant-Based Fish Sauce

MAKES: 3 to 4 cups | **PREP TIME:** 10 minutes, plus 8 hours to steep
COOK TIME: 20 minutes

Fish sauce is a staple ingredient in Thai and Vietnamese cooking. I always have a bottle of this plant-based version on hand for when I get a hankering for Shiitake, Lemongrass, and Rice Noodle Pho (page 78) or when I need to get a briny, umami sea-like flavor, such as in my Lobster-Less Bisque (page 74). I save and sanitize used vinegar bottles to store this plant-based fish sauce in the refrigerator, where it lasts for several weeks. Find the kombu, also known as kelp, in an Asian market or online.

4 cups water

1 (4-by-8-inch) sheet of kombu

½ cup dried shiitake mushrooms

¼ cup low-sodium soy sauce, tamari, or coconut aminos

3 garlic cloves, crushed

2 teaspoons rice vinegar

1. In a medium saucepan, combine the water, kombu, mushrooms, soy sauce, garlic, and vinegar. Bring the mixture to a boil, then reduce the heat to low.

2. Cover and simmer for 15 to 20 minutes. Remove from the heat. Keep covered and allow to steep overnight or for at least 8 hours.

3. Strain and discard any solids. Store the plant-based fish sauce in the refrigerator in a glass bottle for up to 3 weeks, shaking well before each use.

Per serving (1 tablespoon): Calories: 2; Fat: 0g; Carbohydrates: <1g; Protein: <1g; Fiber: <1g; Sodium: 52mg

Nut-free

Plant-Based Worcestershire Sauce

MAKES: about ¾ cup | **PREP TIME:** 5 minutes | **COOK TIME:** 20 minutes

Many people new to plant-based eating don't realize that traditional Worcestershire sauce is made with anchovies, which means it's not plant-based. This version is 100 percent WFPBSOS compliant and is delicious used as a condiment or as a component in sauces, stews, soups, and entrées such as Mama's Mighty Meatless Award-Winning Chili (page 90), Irish Stout Stew (page 85), or SOS-Free BBQ Sauce (page 140).

1 cup apple
   cider vinegar

¼ cup low-sodium
   soy sauce, tamari, or
   coconut aminos

2 tablespoons
   maple syrup

2 tablespoons
   Plant-Based Fish
   Sauce (page 138) or
   store-bought

1 teaspoon
   ground ginger

1 teaspoon dry mustard

1 teaspoon
   onion powder

¼ teaspoon ground
   cinnamon

¼ teaspoon ground
   black pepper

¼ teaspoon ground
   allspice, or
   3 berries, crushed

1 garlic clove, crushed

1. In a medium saucepan, combine the vinegar, soy sauce, maple syrup, fish sauce, ginger, mustard, onion powder, cinnamon, pepper, allspice, and garlic.

2. Bring to a boil over high heat, then lower the heat to medium-low. Simmer for 15 to 20 minutes, until reduced by half.

3. Strain and discard any solids. Store the sauce in the refrigerator in a glass bottle for up to 3 months, shaking well before each use.

Per serving (1 tablespoon): Calories: 19; Fat: <1g; Carbohydrates: 3g; Protein: 1g; Fiber: <1g; Sodium: 264mg

Nut-free

SOS-Free BBQ Sauce

MAKES: about 3 to 4 cups | **PREP TIME:** 20 minutes

One of the challenges with finding a great BBQ sauce is the amount of sugar and salt in most store-bought varieties, not to mention other unhealthy or less-than-natural ingredients. When you make your own, you can feel good about slathering it on anything you like, including using it to make BBQ Pulled Jackfruit Sandwiches (page 107). This BBQ sauce is sweetened with dates and (surprisingly) blueberries, which lend it a deep, rich color but don't overpower the sauce with a berry flavor.

7 pitted dates, chopped

1¼ cups water

¼ cup fresh or frozen blueberries

1 tablespoon Plant-Based Worcestershire Sauce (page 139) or store-bought

1 tablespoon apple cider vinegar

1 (15-ounce) can tomato sauce

2 teaspoons garlic powder

1 teaspoon paprika

1 teaspoon onion powder

½ teaspoon ground allspice

½ teaspoon dry mustard

12 grinds ground black pepper

1. Put the dates in a blender or food processor. Cover them with the water. Let them soak to soften for 15 minutes.

2. Add the blueberries, Worcestershire sauce, vinegar, tomato sauce, garlic powder, paprika, onion powder, allspice, mustard, and black pepper. Blend or process on high until the sauce is smooth, stopping to scrape down the sides as needed. Store in a glass container in the refrigerator for up to 3 weeks.

Per serving (½ cup): Calories: 55; Fat: <1g; Carbohydrates: 13g; Protein: 2g; Fiber: 2g; Sodium: 399mg

Gluten-free

20-Minute Cashew Cheeze Sauce

MAKES: about 3 cups | **PREP TIME:** 5 minutes, plus 1 hour to soak
COOK TIME: 15 minutes

You can stir this into any dish that requires a cheese alternative like Garlic Lovers' Chili Mac and Cheeze (page 115) or Cheezy Broccoli and Rice Casserole (page 98), or use it as a sauce over baked potatoes, for dipping veggies or tortilla chips, or in any other instance that could benefit from cheezy goodness.

½ cup raw cashews

1 cup peeled and diced potatoes

¼ cup diced carrots

¼ cup diced onions

3 cups water

4 tablespoons nutritional yeast

1 tablespoon lemon juice

1 teaspoon miso paste

½ teaspoon garlic powder

½ teaspoon dry mustard

Pinch paprika

Ground black pepper

Salt (optional)

1. Soak the cashews for 30 to 60 minutes in very hot (boiled) water before use in order for your sauce to be creamy and delicious. You can omit this step if you have a high-speed blender.

2. In a medium pot, combine the potatoes, carrots, and onion and cover with the water. Bring to a boil and cook for about 15 minutes, until the vegetables are tender and easily mushed with a fork.

3. While the vegetables are boiling, drain the cashews if you soaked them. Transfer them to a blender or food processor and add the nutritional yeast, lemon juice, miso paste, garlic powder, mustard, and paprika. Season with pepper and salt (if using).

4. When the vegetables are cooked, reserve 1 cup of cooking water and add it to the blender along with the cooked vegetables. Blend for 30 to 60 seconds, until smooth. This will keep for up to 4 days in the refrigerator.

Per serving (¼ cup): Calories: 55; Fat: 3g; Carbohydrates: 6g; Protein: 3g; Fiber: 1g; Sodium: 23mg

Gluten-free, Nut-free, Soy-free

10-Minute White Bean Cheeze Sauce

MAKES: about 3 cups | **PREP TIME:** 10 minutes

If you need a cheeze sauce that is nut-free, soy-free, and gluten-free, this white bean version will meet your needs deliciously.

1 cup canned white beans, drained and rinsed

½ cup unsweetened plant-based milk

5 tablespoons nutritional yeast

¼ teaspoon garlic powder

½ teaspoon apple cider vinegar

1 teaspoon Dijon mustard

¼ teaspoon paprika

¼ teaspoon ground turmeric

Salt (optional)

1. Place the beans, milk, nutritional yeast, garlic powder, vinegar, mustard, paprika, and turmeric in a blender or food processor. Season with salt (if using). Blend for 30 to 60 seconds, until creamy.

2. Heat the sauce on the stove or in the microwave. This will keep for up to 4 days in the refrigerator.

Per serving (¼ cup): Calories: 32; Fat: <1g; Carbohydrates: 4g; Protein: 3g; Fiber: 2g; Sodium: 25mg

Gluten-free, Nut-free

5-Minute Tofu Cheeze Sauce

MAKES: about 2 cups | **PREP TIME:** 5 minutes

When you have a nut allergy and need a creamy cheeze sauce, or if you're short on time, try this five-minute tofu version. It gets a distinctive tanginess from the combination of white wine vinegar and Dijon mustard and has even more protein than the cashew version.

1 (12-ounce) package
   silken tofu

½ cup nutritional yeast

1½ teaspoons
   onion powder

½ teaspoon
   garlic powder

¼ teaspoon paprika

2 teaspoons
   Dijon mustard

1 tablespoon white
   wine vinegar

1 teaspoon salt
   (optional)

½ cup unsweetened
   plant-based milk

1. Place the tofu, nutritional yeast, onion powder, garlic powder, paprika, mustard, vinegar, salt (if using), and milk into a blender or food processor. Blend for 30 to 60 seconds, until well combined.

2. Heat the sauce on the stove or in the microwave. This will keep for up to 4 days in the refrigerator.

Per serving (¼ cup): Calories: 54; Fat: 2g; Carbohydrates: 4g; Protein: 7g; Fiber: 2g; Sodium: 51mg

Gluten-free, Nut-free, Soy-free

Oil-Free Hummus

MAKES: about 2 cups | **PREP TIME:** 10 minutes

Hummus has been around for centuries, originating in the Middle East, although no historians can say categorically which culture we can thank for this smooth, creamy blend of chickpeas, sesame seeds, lemon juice, and garlic. Many recipes use copious amounts of olive oil, but this version gets its oil from raw sesame seeds. Easy, fast, and delicious, you can use this as a dip for raw veggies, dollop it on top of salads or rice bowls, or use it as a sandwich or wrap spread.

1 (15-ounce) can chickpeas, undrained

¼ cup raw sesame seeds

4 garlic cloves

Juice from ½ lemon

¾ teaspoon ground cumin

¼ teaspoon paprika

½ teaspoon salt (optional)

Put the chickpeas and about half of the liquid from the can in a blender or food processor. Add the sesame seeds, garlic, lemon juice, cumin, paprika, and salt (if using). Blend until creamy. Store in the refrigerator for up to 3 days.

Per serving (2 tablespoons): Calories: 40; Fat: 2g; Carbohydrates: 4g; Protein: 2g; Fiber: 1g; Sodium: 37mg

Gluten-free, Nut-free, Soy-free

Greener Guacamole

MAKES: 1 to 1½ cups | **PREP TIME:** 15 minutes

Upon seeing the name of this recipe, you might be wondering why I call this "greener" guacamole. Isn't all guacamole green? Well, yes, but my version uses almost exclusively green ingredients—avocados, lime juice, and scallions (aka green onions)—and leaves out the tomatoes. I love mine mashed with a fork and a little chunky. The acid from the lime juice in this recipe adds a nice touch and cuts through the healthy fat of the avocado.

2 ripe avocados, pitted, peeled, and diced

Juice of ½ lime

2 scallions, green and white parts, chopped

1 garlic clove, minced

½ teaspoon ground cumin

½ small bunch cilantro, chopped

Ground black pepper

Salt (optional)

In a medium bowl, combine the avocados, lime juice, scallions, garlic, cumin, cilantro, pepper, and salt (if using). Mash together with a fork to the desired consistency. Transfer to a serving bowl and chill until serving.

INGREDIENT TIP: Shopping for avocados doesn't have to be tricky. Look for a firm black fruit that gives ever so slightly when pressed. If the avocados at your grocery store are hard as rocks (which is often the case), choose any avocado and allow it to ripen on the counter, or speed things up by placing it in a paper bag with another piece of fruit, like an apple or a banana. The ethylene gas from the fruit will help ripen the avocado. Check it daily, and when it softens, place it in the refrigerator, where it will keep for a few days, or use it right away.

Per serving (2 tablespoons): Calories: 40; Fat: 4g; Carbohydrates: 3g; Protein: 1g; Fiber: 2g; Sodium: 3mg

Gluten-free, Nut-free

Shredded Tofu Meaty Crumbles

MAKES: about 1½ cups | **PREP TIME:** 10 minutes | **COOK TIME:** 45 minutes

When I discovered this amazing substitute and used it in a recipe for the first time, I was hooked. This is a game-changer if you're looking for a toothsome, meaty texture to add to stews, soups, and sauces. See the variations for some flavor profiles to try. Use the BBQ crumbles to top Cheezy Stuffed Potato Skins (page 42) or as a mix-in with the Buffalo Cauliflower Dip (page 35). Sprinkle the Italian-inspired crumbles into Minestrone Soup (page 71), or try the Indian-inspired crumbles in the Green Lentil and Potato Dal (page 99).

FOR THE CRUMBLES

1 (14-ounce) package extra-firm tofu, drained

1 tablespoon Low-Sodium Vegetable Broth (page 136) or store-bought

1 tablespoon low-sodium soy sauce, tamari, or coconut aminos

1 recipe Seasoning Blend, or 3 teaspoons store-bought seasoning of choice

SEASONING BLEND OPTIONS

BBQ

1 teaspoon paprika

¾ teaspoon garlic powder

½ teaspoon onion powder

½ teaspoon ground cumin

ITALIAN-INSPIRED

Substitute 1 tablespoon balsamic vinegar for soy sauce

1 teaspoon garlic powder

¾ teaspoon onion powder

¾ teaspoon dried oregano

½ teaspoon dried basil

INDIAN-INSPIRED

1 teaspoon garlic powder

½ teaspoon ground turmeric

½ teaspoon garam masala

½ teaspoon dry mustard

½ teaspoon ground cumin

1. Preheat the oven to 350°F. Line a rimmed baking sheet with a silicone baking mat, aluminum foil, or parchment paper. Set aside.

2. Make the crumbles: Using the medium-coarse side of a box grater, grate the tofu and put it in a medium bowl. Add the broth, soy sauce, and seasoning mixture and gently stir to combine. Spread in a single layer on the prepared baking sheet.

3. Bake for 15 minutes. Remove from the oven, stir, and bake for another 15 minutes. Stir again and bake for a final 10 to 15 minutes. The finished product should be slightly brown, very dry, and chewy.

4. Allow to cool and use in any recipe where you would want a shredded meaty texture. Store in the refrigerator for up to 3 days.

Per serving (¾ cup): Calories: 200; Fat: 10g; Carbohydrates: 9g; Protein: 22g; Fiber: 4g; Sodium: 348mg

Gluten-free, Nut-free, Soy-free, Freezable

Chipotle Peppers in Adobo Sauce

MAKES: 20 to 25 peppers | **PREP TIME:** 30 minutes, plus 30 minutes to soak
COOK TIME: 20 minutes

These spicy flavor bombs are a cornerstone of Mexican and Southwestern cooking. Yes, you can buy them canned in any grocery store, but they are always made with salt, sugar, and oil. While this recipe is long, each step is simple (roasting, soaking, sautéing, blending, and simmering), and I promise the result is worth the effort. Plus, each batch can last for a month in the refrigerator or up to 6 months in the freezer.

1 (2-ounce) package morita chiles (about 17 to 20)

1 (2-ounce) package chipotle chiles (about 10 to 12)

1 to 2 cups boiling water

½ onion, chopped

1 garlic clove, crushed

½ teaspoon ground cumin

½ teaspoon dried oregano

½ teaspoon dried marjoram

¼ cup apple cider vinegar

¼ cup rice vinegar

2 tablespoons Date Syrup (page 134) or preferred sweetener

2 tablespoons tomato paste

1. Preheat the oven to 350°F. Line a baking sheet with aluminum foil. Place the morita and chipotle chiles on the prepared baking sheet and roast for 5 minutes. Then place them in a medium glass bowl and cover with the boiling water. Use a small plate or bowl to submerge the chiles and let them soak to rehydrate for 30 minutes.

2. Meanwhile, in a nonstick skillet over medium-high heat, dry sauté the onion for about 5 minutes, adding 1 teaspoon of water as needed to prevent sticking, until it is translucent. Add the garlic, cumin, oregano, and marjoram and sauté for 1 more minute, until fragrant. Remove from heat.

3. Transfer the onion mixture to a blender. Add the apple cider vinegar, rice vinegar, date syrup, and tomato paste. After the chiles are rehydrated, remove the stem from 6 to 7 of the morita chiles and, using a paring knife, slice them open to scrape out the seeds. Add the scraped chiles to the blender along with ¾ cup of their soaking liquid. Blend well. Discard any leftover liquid.

4. Pour the sauce back into the skillet and add the remaining chiles. Cook over medium heat, stirring occasionally, for 15 minutes, until the sauce is reduced by half.

Per serving (1 pepper): Calories: 30; Fat: 0g; Carbohydrates: 6g; Protein: 1g; Fiber: 2g; Sodium: 6mg

INGREDIENT TIP: For this recipe, using these exact varieties of peppers is important. They'll usually be stocked at Mexican, Indian, or Asian markets or can be ordered online. Wear gloves when prepping them or be sure to wash your hands well. The oils will burn your eyes if you happen to rub them.

Gluten-free, Nut-free, Soy-free, Freezable

Mama Mia Marinara Sauce

MAKES: about 7 cups | **PREP TIME:** 10 minutes | **COOK TIME:** 2 to 3 hours on High or 4 to 5 hours on Low

When you make a pot of this delicious marinara sauce, you can enjoy it as a pasta sauce, as a pizza sauce, and as the beginning of a fabulous meal, such as Spinach Lasagna (page 116). It freezes beautifully, so I always make as much as my pot can hold. The benefit of making your own is that you control the ingredients and don't have any of the hidden salt, sugar, or oil present in most store-bought jars of marinara sauce.

1 medium onion, diced

5 garlic cloves, minced

2 (28-ounce) cans
no-salt-added
crushed tomatoes

½ cup red wine

2 tablespoons Italian
seasoning, or
1 tablespoon each
dried basil and
dried oregano

Ground black pepper

Salt (optional)

1. Put the onion, garlic, and tomatoes in the slow cooker. Swirl the wine in the empty tomato cans and pour everything into the slow cooker. Add the Italian seasoning, pepper, and salt (if using). Stir to combine.

2. Cover and cook on High for 2 to 3 hours or on Low for 4 to 5 hours.

Per serving (½ cup): Calories: 30; Fat: 0g; Carbohydrates: 4g; Protein: 1g; Fiber: 1g; Sodium: 1mg

VARIATION TIP: You can also cook this marinara sauce in a large pot on the stove. Dry sauté the onion for a few minutes, adding a little water as needed to keep the onion from sticking. Then add the garlic and sauté for 30 seconds and add the remaining ingredients. Bring to a boil, lower the heat, and simmer for about 30 minutes, stirring occasionally.

QUICK REFERENCE COOKING GUIDE

VEGETABLE (AMOUNT)	PREP	ADDITIONAL INGREDIENTS
DRIED BLACK BEANS (1-POUND BAG)	Rinse and sort	2 bay leaves, 1 small quartered onion, boiling water to cover beans by 2 inches
DRIED BLACK-EYED PEAS (1-POUND BAG)	Rinse and sort	Boiling water to cover beans by 2 inches
DRIED CANNELLINI BEANS (1-POUND BAG)	Rinse and sort, soak for 60 to 90 minutes	Boiling water to cover beans by 2 inches
DRIED CHICKPEAS (1-POUND BAG)	Rinse and sort	7 cups water, ¼ teaspoon baking soda
DRIED KIDNEY BEANS (1-POUND BAG)	Rinse and sort, boil in water for 10 minutes, drain and rinse	Boiling water to cover beans by 2 inches
DRIED NAVY BEANS (1-POUND BAG)	Rinse and sort	Boiling water to cover beans by 2 inches
DRIED PINTO BEANS (1-POUND BAG)	Rinse and sort	Boiling water to cover beans by 2 inches
SWEET POTATOES (WHOLE)	Scrub, drip dry, prick with a fork (no need to fully dry or wrap)	N/A
BAKED POTATOES	Scrub, dry, prick with a fork, wrap in foil	Rub with oil and salt (optional)
BEETS	Remove greens, scrub, wrap in foil; after cooking and cooling remove skins	Rub with oil and salt (optional)
GARLIC	Cut off top ¼ inch, wrap in foil; after cooking remove from skins	Drizzle with olive oil (optional)
BELL PEPPERS	Wash, remove stems and seeds, quarter; after cooking peel off skins	N/A

COOK TIME	YIELD (CUPS)	NOTE
3 to 4 hours on High 6 to 8 hours on Low	5 to 6 cups	There are about 2 cups in one can of cooked beans. Store cooked beans in one of two ways: (1) drained, patted dry, and frozen in an airtight container (I use a resealable freezer bag and store them in 2-cup packets) or (2) with their cooking liquid and refrigerated in a resealable container for up to 3 days.
3 to 4 hours on High 6 to 8 hours on Low	5 to 6 cups	
3 hours on High, then 3 to 4 hours on Low	4 to 5 cups	
4 hours on High 8 to 9 hours on Low	5 to 6 cups	
3 hours on High, then 3 to 4 hours on Low	4 to 5 cups	
3 to 4 hours on High 6 to 8 hours on Low	6 cups	
3 to 4 hours on High 6 to 8 hours on Low	6 cups	
3 to 4 hours on High 6 to 7 hours on Low	N/A	
4 to 5 hours on High 8 to 10 hours on Low	N/A	
3 to 4 hours on High 7 to 8 hours on Low	N/A	
2 to 3 hours on High 4 to 5 hours on Low	N/A	
2 hours on High 3 to 4 hours on Low	N/A	

MEASUREMENT CONVERSIONS

	US STANDARD	US STANDARD (OUNCES)	METRIC (APPROXIMATE)
VOLUME EQUIVALENTS (LIQUID)	2 tablespoons	1 fl. oz.	30 mL
	¼ cup	2 fl. oz.	60 mL
	½ cup	4 fl. oz.	120 mL
	1 cup	8 fl. oz.	240 mL
	1½ cups	12 fl. oz.	355 mL
	2 cups or 1 pint	16 fl. oz.	475 mL
	4 cups or 1 quart	32 fl. oz.	1 L
	1 gallon	128 fl. oz.	4 L
VOLUME EQUIVALENTS (DRY)	⅛ teaspoon	——————	0.5 mL
	¼ teaspoon	——————	1 mL
	½ teaspoon	——————	2 mL
	¾ teaspoon	——————	4 mL
	1 teaspoon	——————	5 mL
	1 tablespoon	——————	15 mL
	¼ cup	——————	59 mL
	⅓ cup	——————	79 mL
	½ cup	——————	118 mL
	⅔ cup	——————	156 mL
	¾ cup	——————	177 mL
	1 cup	——————	235 mL
	2 cups or 1 pint	——————	475 mL
	3 cups	——————	700 mL
	4 cups or 1 quart	——————	1 L
	½ gallon	——————	2 L
	1 gallon	——————	4 L
WEIGHT EQUIVALENTS	½ ounce	——————	15 g
	1 ounce	——————	30 g
	2 ounces	——————	60 g
	4 ounces	——————	115 g
	8 ounces	——————	225 g
	12 ounces	——————	340 g
	16 ounces or 1 pound	——————	455 g

	FAHRENHEIT (F)	CELSIUS (C) (APPROXIMATE)
OVEN TEMPERATURES	250°F	120°C
	300°F	150°C
	325°F	180°C
	375°F	190°C
	400°F	200°C
	425°F	220°C
	450°F	230°C

RESOURCES AND REFERENCES

Books

Eat for Life by Joel Fuhrman (2020)

How Not to Die: Discover the Foods Scientifically Proven to Prevent and Reverse Disease by Michael Greger and Gene Stone (2015)

How Not to Diet: The Groundbreaking Science of Healthy, Permanent Weight Loss by Michael Greger (2019)

Prevent and Reverse Heart Disease: The Revolutionary, Scientifically Proven, Nutrition-Based Cure by Caldwell B. Esselstyn (2008)

The China Study: Revised and Expanded Edition: The Most Comprehensive Study of Nutrition Ever Conducted and the Startling Implications for Diet, Weight Loss, and Long-Term Health by T. Colin Campbell and Thomas M. Campbell II (2016)

The Starch Solution by John McDougall (2013)

Whole: Rethinking the Science of Nutrition by T. Colin Campbell and Howard Jacobson (2014)

Documentaries

Forks Over Knives

PlantPure Nation

The Game Changers

What the Health

INDEX

A

Allergens, 14
Appetizers. *See* Snacks
    and appetizers
Apples
  "Here Comes Autumn"
    Apple Crisp, 128–129
  Maple, Apple, and Walnut
    Great Grains, 20
  Tangy Cabbage, Apples,
    and Potatoes, 94
Apricot Pilaf, Ginger, Shiitake,
    Pecan and, 51
Artichoke Dip, Spinach-, 32–33

B

Barley
  Mushroom and Barley
    Stew, 88
  Three Bean and Barley
    White Chili, 89
BBQ Black Beans and
    Sweet Potatoes, 101
BBQ Pulled Jackfruit
    Sandwiches, 107
BBQ Sauce, SOS-Free, 140
Beans, 9
  BBQ Black Beans and
    Sweet Potatoes, 101
  Black Bean, Corn, and
    Salsa Fiesta, 111
  British Beans on Toast, 24
  Cajun-Style Red Beans
    and Rice, 50
  cooking guide, 152–153
  Creamy Southwestern
    Salsa Bean Dip, 36
  Kale and White Bean
    Soup, 73

Mama's Mighty Meatless
    Award-Winning
    Chili, 90–91
  Minestrone Soup, 71
  Spicy Black Bean Soup, 61
  Sweet Potato, Red Beans,
    and Lentil Stew, 83
  Sweet Potato and Black
    Bean Hash, 25
  10-Minute White Bean
    Cheeze Sauce, 142
  Three Bean and Barley
    White Chili, 89
  White Bean Tzatziki
    Dip, 34
Beet Salad with Walnuts
    and Dijon-Maple
    Dressing, Rosemary-
    and-Garlic, 46–47
Bell peppers
  cooking guide, 152–153
  Deconstructed Stuffed
    Pepper Stew, 87
  Green Pepper, Potato, and
    Mushroom Scallopini
    Sandwiches, 108–109
  Hawaiian-Inspired Pepper
    Pot with Brown Rice, 113
  Portobello Mushroom
    Fajitas, 105
  Roasted Red Pepper and
    Romaine Salad with
    Green Olives and
    Tomatoes, 48
Berries
  Blueberry, Cinnamon, and
    Pecan French Toast, 22
  Strawberries and Cream
    Overnight Oatmeal, 21
Black Bean, Corn, and
    Salsa Fiesta, 111

Black-Eyed Peas and Collard
    Greens with Brown Rice, 95
Blueberry, Cinnamon, and
    Pecan French Toast, 22
British Beans on Toast, 24
Broccoli and Rice Casserole,
    Cheezy, 98
Broth, Low-Sodium
    Vegetable, 136
Brownies, Chocolate's
    Best Friends, 122
Bruschetta, Eggplant
    Caponata, 37
Brussels Sprouts with
    Dates and Pecans,
    Maple-Glazed Butternut
    Squash and, 55
Buffalo Cauliflower Dip, 35
Burritos, Southwestern-
    Style Breakfast, 26
Butternut squash
  Butternut Squash Soup, 70
  Maple-Glazed Butternut
    Squash and Brussels
    Sprouts with Dates
    and Pecans, 55
  Sweet and Savory Root
    Veggies and Butternut
    Squash, 103

C

Cabbage
  Irish Stout Stew, 85
  Tangy Cabbage, Apples,
    and Potatoes, 94
  Thai-Inspired Coconut
    Cabbage Soup, 68–69
Cajun-Style Jambalaya, 114
Cajun-Style Red Beans
    and Rice, 50

Cakes
  Gooey Bittersweet
    Chocolate Pudding
    Cake, 124–125
  Lemon Poppy Seed
    Cake, 130–131
  Poppy's Carrot Cake, 126–127
Carrots
  Poppy's Carrot Cake, 126–127
  Spiced Glazed Carrots, 40
Cashew Cheeze Sauce,
  20-Minute, 141
Casseroles
  Cheezy Broccoli and
    Rice Casserole, 98
  Potato and Veggie Breakfast
    Casserole, 23
Cauliflower
  Buffalo Cauliflower Dip, 35
  Cauliflower, Chickpea, Quinoa,
    and Coconut Curry, 77
Cheeze sauces
  5-Minute Tofu Cheeze
    Sauce, 143
  10-Minute White Bean
    Cheeze Sauce, 142
  20-Minute Cashew
    Cheeze Sauce, 141
Cheezy Broccoli and Rice
  Casserole, 98
Cheezy Stuffed Potato
  Skins, 42–43
Chickpeas
  Cauliflower, Chickpea, Quinoa,
    and Coconut Curry, 77
  Chickpea, Kale, and
    Lentil Stew, 84
  Chickpea Noodle Soup, 65
  Chickpea of the Sea
    Salad, 56
  cooking guide, 152–153
  Crispy Chickpea Snackers, 39
  Oil-Free Hummus, 144
Chili-Lime Corn, 52
Chili Powder, 135

Chilis. *See* Soups, stews,
  and chilis
Chipotle Peppers in Adobo
  Sauce, 148–149
Chocolate
  Chocolate's Best Friends
    Brownies, 122
  Gooey Bittersweet
    Chocolate Pudding
    Cake, 124–125
Chowders. *See* Soups,
  stews, and chilis
Classic Italian Mushrooms, 41
Cobbler, Peach, 123
Coconut and coconut milk
  allergen note, 14
  Cauliflower, Chickpea,
    Quinoa, and Coconut
    Curry, 77
  Thai-Inspired Coconut
    Cabbage Soup, 68–69
Collard Greens with Brown
  Rice, Black-Eyed
  Peas and, 95
Comforting Tomato
  Soup, 60
Corn
  Black Bean, Corn, and
    Salsa Fiesta, 111
  Chili-Lime Corn, 52
  Creamy Corn Chowder, 81
Creamy Corn Chowder, 81
Creamy Dreamy Brown
  Rice Pudding, 120
Creamy Orzo with
  Wheatberries, Raisins,
  and Swiss Chard, 100
Creamy Southwestern
  Salsa Bean Dip, 36
Crisp, "Here Comes Autumn"
  Apple, 128–129
Crispy Chickpea Snackers, 39
Curried Zucchini Soup, 63
Curry, Cauliflower, Chickpea,
  Quinoa, and Coconut, 77

D
Dairy alternatives, 10
Dates
  Date Syrup, 134
  Maple-Glazed Butternut
    Squash and Brussels
    Sprouts with Dates
    and Pecans, 55
Deconstructed Stuffed
  Pepper Stew, 87
Desserts
  Chocolate's Best Friends
    Brownies, 122
  Creamy Dreamy Brown
    Rice Pudding, 120
  Gooey Bittersweet
    Chocolate Pudding
    Cake, 124–125
  "Here Comes Autumn"
    Apple Crisp, 128–129
  Lemon Poppy Seed
    Cake, 130–131
  Peach Cobbler, 123
  Poppy's Carrot Cake, 126–127
  Pumpkin Pie Oatmeal
    Parfaits, 121
Dijon-Maple Dressing,
  Rosemary-and-Garlic
  Beet Salad with
  Walnuts and, 46–47
Dips and spreads
  Buffalo Cauliflower
    Dip, 35
  Creamy Southwestern
    Salsa Bean Dip, 36
  Greener Guacamole, 145
  Oil-Free Hummus, 144
  Pineapple, Peach, and
    Mango Salsa, 31
  Rosemary-Onion Jam, 30
  Spinach-Artichoke
    Dip, 32–33
  White Bean Tzatziki
    Dip, 34

E

Egg alternatives, 10
Eggplants
    Eggplant Caponata
        Bruschetta, 37
    Ratatouille, 102

F

Fajitas, Portobello
    Mushroom, 105
Fish Sauce, Plant-Based, 138
5-Minute Tofu Cheeze
    Sauce, 143
Freezable
    British Beans on Toast, 24
    Butternut Squash Soup, 70
    Chickpea, Kale, and
        Lentil Stew, 84
    Chickpea Noodle Soup, 65
    Chili-Lime Corn, 52
    Chipotle Peppers in Adobo
        Sauce, 148–149
    Comforting Tomato Soup, 60
    Creamy Corn Chowder, 81
    Crispy Chickpea Snackers, 39
    Curried Zucchini Soup, 63
    Deconstructed Stuffed
        Pepper Stew, 87
    French Onion Soup, 64
    Golden Split Pea Soup, 67
    Hearty Potato, Tomato, and
        Green Beans Stufato, 80
    Irish Stout Stew, 85
    Italian Lentil Soup, 72
    Kale and White Bean Soup, 73
    Lentil Sloppy Joes, 110
    Low-Sodium Vegetable
        Broth, 136
    Mama Mia Marinara
        Sauce, 150
    Mama's Mighty Meatless
        Award-Winning
        Chili, 90–91
    Minestrone Soup, 71

Mushroom and Barley
    Stew, 88
Old-Fashioned Beefless
    Stew, 86
Potato-Leek Soup, 62
Shiitake, Lemongrass, and
    Rice Noodle Pho, 78–79
Southwestern-Style
    Breakfast Burritos, 26
Spicy Black Bean Soup, 61
Sweet Potato, Red Beans,
    and Lentil Stew, 83
Three Bean and Barley
    White Chili, 89
French Onion Soup, 64
French Toast, Blueberry,
    Cinnamon, and Pecan, 22
Fruits, 12. See also specific
    Nutty Granola with
        Power Seeds and
        Dried Fruit, 18–19

G

Garlic
    Garlic Lovers' Chili Mac
        and Cheeze, 115
    Garlic Mashed Potatoes, 54
    Rosemary-and-Garlic Beet
        Salad with Walnuts
        and Dijon-Maple
        Dressing, 46–47
Ginger, Shiitake, Pecan, and
    Apricot Pilaf, 51
Gluten-free
    Black Bean, Corn, and
        Salsa Fiesta, 111
    Black-Eyed Peas and Collard
        Greens with Brown Rice, 95
    Buffalo Cauliflower Dip, 35
    Butternut Squash Soup, 70
    Cajun-Style Jambalaya, 114
    Cajun-Style Red Beans
        and Rice, 50
    Cauliflower, Chickpea, Quinoa,
        and Coconut Curry, 77

Cheezy Broccoli and
    Rice Casserole, 98
Cheezy Stuffed Potato
    Skins, 42–43
Chickpea, Kale, and
    Lentil Stew, 84
Chickpea of the Sea Salad, 56
Chili-Lime Corn, 52
Chili Powder, 135
Chipotle Peppers in Adobo
    Sauce, 148–149
Chocolate's Best Friends
    Brownies, 122
Classic Italian Mushrooms, 41
Comforting Tomato Soup, 60
Creamy Corn Chowder, 81
Creamy Dreamy Brown
    Rice Pudding, 120
Creamy Southwestern
    Salsa Bean Dip, 36
Crispy Chickpea Snackers, 39
Curried Zucchini Soup, 63
Date Syrup, 134
Deconstructed Stuffed
    Pepper Stew, 87
5-Minute Tofu Cheeze
    Sauce, 143
Garlic Mashed Potatoes, 54
Ginger, Shiitake, Pecan,
    and Apricot Pilaf, 51
Golden Split Pea Soup, 67
Greener Guacamole, 145
Green Lentil and
    Potato Dal, 99
Hearty Potato, Tomato, and
    Green Beans Stufato, 80
"Here Comes Autumn"
    Apple Crisp, 128–129
Italian Lentil Soup, 72
Kale and White Bean Soup, 73
Low-Sodium Vegetable
    Broth, 136
Mama Mia Marinara Sauce, 150

Maple-Glazed Butternut
    Squash and Brussels
    Sprouts with Dates
    and Pecans, 55
Nutty Granola with
    Power Seeds and
    Dried Fruit, 18–19
Oil-Free Hummus, 144
Peach Cobbler, 123
Pineapple, Peach, and
    Mango Salsa, 31
Plant-Based Parmesan, 137
Poppy's Carrot Cake, 126–127
Potato and Veggie Breakfast
    Casserole, 23
Potato-Leek Soup, 62
Pumpkin Pie Oatmeal
    Parfaits, 121
Ratatouille, 102
Roasted Red Pepper and
    Romaine Salad with Green
    Olives and Tomatoes, 48
Rosemary-and-Garlic Beet
    Salad with Walnuts
    and Dijon-Maple
    Dressing, 46–47
Rosemary-Onion Jam, 30
Shredded Tofu Meaty
    Crumbles, 146–147
Southwestern Quinoa
    Taco Bowls, 112
Spiced Glazed Carrots, 40
Strawberries and Cream
    Overnight Oatmeal, 21
Sweet and Savory Root
    Veggies and Butternut
    Squash, 103
Sweet 'n' Spicy Crunchy
    Snack Mix, 38
Sweet Potato, Red Beans,
    and Lentil Stew, 83
Sweet Potato and Black
    Bean Hash, 25
Tangy Cabbage, Apples,
    and Potatoes, 94

10-Minute White Bean
    Cheeze Sauce, 142
20-Minute Cashew
    Cheeze Sauce, 141
White Bean Tzatziki
    Dip, 34
Golden Split Pea Soup, 67
Gooey Bittersweet Chocolate
    Pudding Cake, 124–125
Grains. See also specific
    Maple, Apple, and Walnut
    Great Grains, 20
Granola with Power Seeds and
    Dried Fruit, Nutty, 18–19
Green Beans Stufato, Hearty
    Potato, Tomato, and, 80
Greener Guacamole, 145
Green Lentil and Potato Dal, 99
Green Pepper, Potato, and
    Mushroom Scallopini
    Sandwiches, 108–109
Greger, Michael, 12
Guacamole, Greener, 145

H

Hawaiian-Inspired Pepper Pot
    with Brown Rice, 113
Hearty Potato, Tomato, and
    Green Beans Stufato, 80
"Here Comes Autumn" Apple
    Crisp, 128–129
Hot and Sour Soup, 76
Hummus, Oil-Free, 144

I

Irish Stout Stew, 85
Italian Lentil Soup, 72

J

Jackfruit Sandwiches,
    BBQ Pulled, 107
Jam, Rosemary-Onion, 30
Jambalaya, Cajun-Style, 114

K

Kale
    Chickpea, Kale, and
        Lentil Stew, 84
    Kale and White Bean Soup, 73

L

Lasagna, Spinach, 116
Leek Soup, Potato-, 62
Lemongrass, and Rice Noodle
    Pho, Shiitake, 78–79
Lemon Poppy Seed
    Cake, 130–131
Lentils
    Chickpea, Kale, and
        Lentil Stew, 84
    Deconstructed Stuffed
        Pepper Stew, 87
    Green Lentil and
        Potato Dal, 99
    Italian Lentil Soup, 72
    Lentil Sloppy Joes, 110
    Sweet Potato, Red Beans,
        and Lentil Stew, 83
Lettuce
    Roasted Red Pepper and
        Romaine Salad with Green
        Olives and Tomatoes, 48
    Shiitake Mushroom and
        Quinoa Lettuce Wraps
        with Peanut Sauce, 96–97
Lime Corn, Chili-, 52
Lobster-Less Bisque, 74–75
Low-Sodium Vegetable
    Broth, 136

M

Mama Mia Marinara Sauce, 150
Mama's Mighty Meatless Award-
    Winning Chili, 90–91
Mango Salsa, Pineapple,
    Peach, and, 31
Maple syrup

Maple, Apple, and Walnut Great Grains, 20
Maple-Glazed Butternut Squash and Brussels Sprouts with Dates and Pecans, 55
Meat alternatives, 10
Meaty Crumbles, Shredded Tofu, 146–147
Milks, plant-based, 11
Minestrone Soup, 71
Mushrooms
Classic Italian Mushrooms, 41
Ginger, Shiitake, Pecan, and Apricot Pilaf, 51
Green Pepper, Potato, and Mushroom Scallopini Sandwiches, 108–109
Hot and Sour Soup, 76
Mushroom and Barley Stew, 88
Mushroom Stroganoff, 104
Old-Fashioned Beefless Stew, 86
Portobello Mushroom Fajitas, 105
Shiitake, Lemongrass, and Rice Noodle Pho, 78–79
Shiitake Mushroom and Quinoa Lettuce Wraps with Peanut Sauce, 96–97
Teriyaki Mushrooms, 53

N

Nachumsohn, Irving, 4
New England No-Clam Chowder, 82
Noodles. See Pasta and noodles
Nut-free and nut-free option
BBQ Black Beans and Sweet Potatoes, 101
BBQ Pulled Jackfruit Sandwiches, 107
Black Bean, Corn, and Salsa Fiesta, 111

Black-Eyed Peas and Collard Greens with Brown Rice, 95
British Beans on Toast, 24
Butternut Squash Soup, 70
Cajun-Style Jambalaya, 114
Cajun-Style Red Beans and Rice, 50
Cauliflower, Chickpea, Quinoa, and Coconut Curry, 77
Cheezy Broccoli and Rice Casserole, 98
Cheezy Stuffed Potato Skins, 42–43
Chickpea, Kale, and Lentil Stew, 84
Chickpea Noodle Soup, 65
Chickpea of the Sea Salad, 56
Chili-Lime Corn, 52
Chili Powder, 135
Chipotle Peppers in Adobo Sauce, 148–149
Chocolate's Best Friends Brownies, 122
Classic Italian Mushrooms, 41
Comforting Tomato Soup, 60
Creamy Corn Chowder, 81
Creamy Dreamy Brown Rice Pudding, 120
Creamy Orzo with Wheatberries, Raisins, and Swiss Chard, 100
Creamy Southwestern Salsa Bean Dip, 36
Crispy Chickpea Snackers, 39
Curried Zucchini Soup, 63
Date Syrup, 134
Deconstructed Stuffed Pepper Stew, 87
Eggplant Caponata Bruschetta, 37
5-Minute Tofu Cheeze Sauce, 143
French Onion Soup, 64
Garlic Lovers' Chili Mac and Cheeze, 115

Garlic Mashed Potatoes, 54
Golden Split Pea Soup, 67
Gooey Bittersweet Chocolate Pudding Cake, 124–125
Greener Guacamole, 145
Green Lentil and Potato Dal, 99
Green Pepper, Potato, and Mushroom Scallopini Sandwiches, 108–109
Hawaiian-Inspired Pepper Pot with Brown Rice, 113
Hearty Potato, Tomato, and Green Beans Stufato, 80
Hot and Sour Soup, 76
Irish Stout Stew, 85
Italian Lentil Soup, 72
Kale and White Bean Soup, 73
Lemon Poppy Seed Cake, 130–131
Lentil Sloppy Joes, 110
Lobster-Less Bisque, 74–75
Low-Sodium Vegetable Broth, 136
Mama Mia Marinara Sauce, 150
Mama's Mighty Meatless Award-Winning Chili, 90–91
Minestrone Soup, 71
Mushroom and Barley Stew, 88
New England No-Clam Chowder, 82
Oil-Free Hummus, 144
Old-Fashioned Beefless Stew, 86
Peach Cobbler, 123
Pineapple, Peach, and Mango Salsa, 31
Plant-Based Fish Sauce, 138
Plant-Based Worcestershire Sauce, 139
Portobello Mushroom Fajitas, 105

Potato and Veggie Breakfast
    Casserole, 23
Ratatouille, 102
Roasted Red Pepper and
    Romaine Salad with
    Green Olives and
    Tomatoes, 48
Rosemary-Onion Jam, 30
Savory Slow Cooker
    Stuffing, 49
Shiitake, Lemongrass,
    and Rice Noodle
    Pho, 78–79
Shredded Tofu Meaty
    Crumbles, 146–147
SOS-Free BBQ
    Sauce, 140
Southwestern Quinoa
    Taco Bowls, 112
Southwestern-Style
    Breakfast Burritos, 26
Spiced Glazed
    Carrots, 40
Spicy Black Bean
    Soup, 61
Strawberries and
    Cream Overnight
    Oatmeal, 21
Sweet and Savory Root
    Veggies and Butternut
    Squash, 103
Sweet Potato, Red Beans,
    and Lentil Stew, 83
Sweet Potato and Black
    Bean Hash, 25
Tangy Cabbage, Apples,
    and Potatoes, 94
10-Minute White Bean
    Cheeze Sauce, 142
Teriyaki Mushrooms, 53
Thai-Inspired
    Coconut Cabbage
    Soup, 68–69
Three Bean and Barley
    White Chili, 89

White Bean Tzatziki Dip, 34
Nuts
    Blueberry, Cinnamon, and
        Pecan French Toast, 22
    Ginger, Shiitake, Pecan,
        and Apricot Pilaf, 51
    Maple, Apple, and Walnut
        Great Grains, 20
    Maple-Glazed Butternut
        Squash and Brussels
        Sprouts with Dates
        and Pecans, 55
    Nutty Granola with
        Power Seeds and
        Dried Fruit, 18–19
    Rosemary-and-Garlic Beet
        Salad with Walnuts
        and Dijon-Maple
        Dressing, 46–47
    Sweet 'n' Spicy Crunchy
        Snack Mix, 38
    20-Minute Cashew
        Cheeze Sauce, 141

O
Oats
    Pumpkin Pie Oatmeal
        Parfaits, 121
    Strawberries and Cream
        Overnight Oatmeal, 21
Oil alternatives, 10
Oil-Free Hummus, 144
Old-Fashioned Beefless
    Stew, 86
Olives and Tomatoes,
    Roasted Red Pepper
    and Romaine Salad
    with Green, 48
Onions
    French Onion Soup, 64
    Rosemary-Onion Jam, 30
Organic foods, 12

P
Pantry staples, 9–10

Parmesan, Plant-Based, 137
Pasta and noodles
    Chickpea Noodle Soup, 65
    Creamy Orzo with
        Wheatberries, Raisins,
        and Swiss Chard, 100
    Garlic Lovers' Chili Mac
        and Cheeze, 115
    Minestrone Soup, 71
    Mushroom Stroganoff, 104
    Shiitake, Lemongrass, and
        Rice Noodle Pho, 78–79
    Spinach Lasagna, 116
Peaches
    Peach Cobbler, 123
    Pineapple, Peach, and
        Mango Salsa, 31
Peanut Sauce, Shiitake
    Mushroom and Quinoa
    Lettuce Wraps with, 96–97
Pecans
    Blueberry, Cinnamon, and
        Pecan French Toast, 22
    Ginger, Shiitake, Pecan,
        and Apricot Pilaf, 51
    Maple-Glazed Butternut
        Squash and Brussels
        Sprouts with Dates
        and Pecans, 55
Pineapple
    Hawaiian-Inspired Pepper
        Pot with Brown Rice, 113
    Pineapple, Peach, and
        Mango Salsa, 31
Plant-based diets, 2–3
Plant-Based Fish Sauce, 138
Plant-Based Parmesan, 137
Plant-Based Worcestershire
    Sauce, 139
Poppy's Carrot Cake, 126–127
Poppy Seed Cake,
    Lemon, 130–131
Portobello Mushroom
    Fajitas, 105

Potatoes. *See also* Sweet potatoes
    Cheezy Stuffed Potato Skins, 42–43
    cooking guide, 152–153
    Garlic Mashed Potatoes, 54
    Green Pepper, Potato, and Mushroom Scallopini Sandwiches, 108–109
    Hearty Potato, Tomato, and Green Beans Stufato, 80
    Irish Stout Stew, 85
    New England No-Clam Chowder, 82
    Old-Fashioned Beefless Stew, 86
    Potato and Veggie Breakfast Casserole, 23
    Potato-Leek Soup, 62
    Sweet and Savory Root Veggies and Butternut Squash, 103
    Tangy Cabbage, Apples, and Potatoes, 94
    Pumpkin Pie Oatmeal Parfaits, 121

Q

Quinoa
    Cauliflower, Chickpea, Quinoa, and Coconut Curry, 77
    Shiitake Mushroom and Quinoa Lettuce Wraps with Peanut Sauce, 96–97
    Southwestern Quinoa Taco Bowls, 112

R

Raisins, and Swiss Chard, Creamy Orzo with Wheatberries, 100
Ratatouille, 102
Recipes, about, 13–14
Rice

Black-Eyed Peas and Collard Greens with Brown Rice, 95
Cajun-Style Red Beans and Rice, 50
Cheezy Broccoli and Rice Casserole, 98
Creamy Dreamy Brown Rice Pudding, 120
Deconstructed Stuffed Pepper Stew, 87
Hawaiian-Inspired Pepper Pot with Brown Rice, 113
Roasted Red Pepper and Romaine Salad with Green Olives and Tomatoes, 48
Rosemary
    Rosemary-and-Garlic Beet Salad with Walnuts and Dijon-Maple Dressing, 46–47
    Rosemary-Onion Jam, 30

S

Safety tips, 6
Salads
    Chickpea of the Sea Salad, 56
    Roasted Red Pepper and Romaine Salad with Green Olives and Tomatoes, 48
    Rosemary-and-Garlic Beet Salad with Walnuts and Dijon-Maple Dressing, 46–47
Salsa
    Black Bean, Corn, and Salsa Fiesta, 111
    Creamy Southwestern Salsa Bean Dip, 36
    Pineapple, Peach, and Mango Salsa, 31
Sandwiches and wraps
    BBQ Pulled Jackfruit Sandwiches, 107

Green Pepper, Potato, and Mushroom Scallopini Sandwiches, 108–109
Lentil Sloppy Joes, 110
Shiitake Mushroom and Quinoa Lettuce Wraps with Peanut Sauce, 96–97
Southwestern-Style Breakfast Burritos, 26
Sauces
    5-Minute Tofu Cheeze Sauce, 143
    Mama Mia Marinara Sauce, 150
    Plant-Based Fish Sauce, 138
    Plant-Based Worcestershire Sauce, 139
    SOS-Free BBQ Sauce, 140
    10-Minute White Bean Cheeze Sauce, 142
    20-Minute Cashew Cheeze Sauce, 141
Savory Slow Cooker Stuffing, 49
Shiitake, Lemongrass, and Rice Noodle Pho, 78–79
Shiitake Mushroom and Quinoa Lettuce Wraps with Peanut Sauce, 96–97
Shredded Tofu Meaty Crumbles, 146–147
Sloppy Joes, Lentil, 110
Slow cookers and cooking
    about, 3–4
    cooking guide, 152–153
    and plant-based diets, 8–9, 11, 13
    safety, 6
    tips, 7
Snacks and appetizers. *See also* Dips and spreads
    Classic Italian Mushrooms, 41
    Crispy Chickpea Snackers, 39
    Eggplant Caponata Bruschetta, 37

Spiced Glazed Carrots, 40

Sweet 'n' Spicy Crunchy
Snack Mix, 38

SOS-Free BBQ Sauce, 140

Soups, stews, and chilis

Butternut Squash Soup, 70

Cauliflower, Chickpea, Quinoa,
and Coconut Curry, 77

Chickpea, Kale, and
Lentil Stew, 84

Chickpea Noodle Soup, 65

Comforting Tomato Soup, 60

Creamy Corn Chowder, 81

Curried Zucchini Soup, 63

Deconstructed Stuffed
Pepper Stew, 87

French Onion Soup, 64

Golden Split Pea Soup, 67

Hearty Potato, Tomato, and
Green Beans Stufato, 80

Hot and Sour Soup, 76

Irish Stout Stew, 85

Italian Lentil Soup, 72

Kale and White Bean Soup, 73

Lobster-Less Bisque, 74–75

Mama's Mighty Meatless
Award-Winning
Chili, 90–91

Minestrone Soup, 71

Mushroom and Barley
Stew, 88

New England No-Clam
Chowder, 82

Old-Fashioned Beefless
Stew, 86

Potato-Leek Soup, 62

Shiitake, Lemongrass, and
Rice Noodle Pho, 78–79

Spicy Black Bean Soup, 61

Sweet Potato, Red Beans,
and Lentil Stew, 83

Thai-Inspired Coconut
Cabbage Soup, 68–69

Three Bean and Barley
White Chili, 89

Southwestern Quinoa
Taco Bowls, 112

Southwestern-Style
Breakfast Burritos, 26

Soy-free

Black Bean, Corn, and
Salsa Fiesta, 111

Black-Eyed Peas and Collard
Greens with Brown Rice, 95

Blueberry, Cinnamon, and
Pecan French Toast, 22

Butternut Squash Soup, 70

Cajun-Style Jambalaya, 114

Cajun-Style Red Beans
and Rice, 50

Cauliflower, Chickpea, Quinoa,
and Coconut Curry, 77

Cheezy Broccoli and
Rice Casserole, 98

Cheezy Stuffed Potato
Skins, 42–43

Chickpea, Kale, and
Lentil Stew, 84

Chickpea Noodle Soup, 65

Chickpea of the Sea Salad, 56

Chili-Lime Corn, 52

Chili Powder, 135

Chipotle Peppers in Adobo
Sauce, 148–149

Chocolate's Best Friends
Brownies, 122

Classic Italian Mushrooms, 41

Comforting Tomato Soup, 60

Creamy Dreamy Brown
Rice Pudding, 120

Creamy Orzo with
Wheatberries, Raisins,
and Swiss Chard, 100

Creamy Southwestern
Salsa Bean Dip, 36

Crispy Chickpea Snackers, 39

Curried Zucchini Soup, 63

Date Syrup, 134

Deconstructed Stuffed
Pepper Stew, 87

Eggplant Caponata
Bruschetta, 37

Garlic Lovers' Chili Mac
and Cheeze, 115

Garlic Mashed Potatoes, 54

Golden Split Pea Soup, 67

Gooey Bittersweet Chocolate
Pudding Cake, 124–125

Greener Guacamole, 145

Green Lentil and
Potato Dal, 99

Green Pepper, Potato, and
Mushroom Scallopini
Sandwiches, 108–109

Hearty Potato, Tomato, and
Green Beans Stufato, 80

"Here Comes Autumn"
Apple Crisp, 128–129

Italian Lentil Soup, 72

Kale and White Bean Soup, 73

Lemon Poppy Seed
Cake, 130–131

Low-Sodium Vegetable
Broth, 136

Mama Mia Marinara
Sauce, 150

Maple, Apple, and Walnut
Great Grains, 20

Maple-Glazed Butternut
Squash and Brussels
Sprouts with Dates
and Pecans, 55

Minestrone Soup, 71

Nutty Granola with
Power Seeds and
Dried Fruit, 18–19

Oil-Free Hummus, 144

Peach Cobbler, 123

Pineapple, Peach, and
Mango Salsa, 31

Plant-Based Parmesan, 137

Poppy's Carrot Cake, 126–127

Portobello Mushroom
Fajitas, 105

Potato-Leek Soup, 62

Soy-free (*continued*)
  Pumpkin Pie Oatmeal
      Parfaits, 121
  Ratatouille, 102
  Roasted Red Pepper and
      Romaine Salad with Green
      Olives and Tomatoes, 48
  Rosemary-and-Garlic Beet
      Salad with Walnuts
      and Dijon-Maple
      Dressing, 46–47
  Rosemary-Onion Jam, 30
  Savory Slow Cooker
      Stuffing, 49
  Southwestern Quinoa
      Taco Bowls, 112
  Spiced Glazed Carrots, 40
  Sweet and Savory Root
      Veggies and Butternut
      Squash, 103
  Sweet Potato, Red Beans,
      and Lentil Stew, 83
  Sweet Potato and Black
      Bean Hash, 25
  Tangy Cabbage, Apples,
      and Potatoes, 94
  10-Minute White Bean
      Cheeze Sauce, 142
  Three Bean and Barley
      White Chili, 89
  White Bean Tzatziki Dip, 34
Spiced Glazed Carrots, 40
Spicy Black Bean Soup, 61
Spinach
  Spinach-Artichoke Dip, 32–33
  Spinach Lasagna, 116
Split Pea Soup, Golden, 67
Stews. *See* Soups, stews,
    and chilis
Strawberries and Cream
    Overnight Oatmeal, 21
Stuffing, Savory Slow
    Cooker, 49
Sweet and Savory Root Veggies
    and Butternut Squash, 103

Sweet 'n' Spicy Crunchy
    Snack Mix, 38
Sweet potatoes
  BBQ Black Beans and
      Sweet Potatoes, 101
  cooking guide, 152–153
  Sweet and Savory Root
      Veggies and Butternut
      Squash, 103
  Sweet Potato, Red Beans,
      and Lentil Stew, 83
  Sweet Potato and Black
      Bean Hash, 25
  Swiss Chard, Creamy Orzo
      with Wheatberries,
      Raisins, and, 100
Syrup, Date, 134

T

Taco Bowls, Southwestern
    Quinoa, 112
Tangy Cabbage, Apples,
    and Potatoes, 94
10-Minute White Bean
    Cheeze Sauce, 142
Teriyaki Mushrooms, 53
Thai-Inspired Coconut
    Cabbage Soup, 68–69
Three Bean and Barley
    White Chili, 89
Tofu
  5-Minute Tofu Cheeze
      Sauce, 143
  Hot and Sour Soup, 76
  Shredded Tofu Meaty
      Crumbles, 146–147
Tomatoes
  Comforting Tomato Soup, 60
  Hearty Potato, Tomato, and
      Green Beans Stufato, 80
  Mama Mia Marinara Sauce, 150
  Roasted Red Pepper and
      Romaine Salad with Green
      Olives and Tomatoes, 48
Tools and equipment, 5

20-Minute Cashew Cheeze
    Sauce, 141
Tzatziki Dip, White Bean, 34

V

Vegan diets, 2
Vegetables, 10, 12. *See also*
    specific
  Low-Sodium Vegetable
      Broth, 136
  Minestrone Soup, 71
  Potato and Veggie Breakfast
      Casserole, 23
  Sweet and Savory Root
      Veggies and Butternut
      Squash, 103

W

Walnuts
  Maple, Apple, and Walnut
      Great Grains, 20
  Rosemary-and-Garlic Beet
      Salad with Walnuts
      and Dijon-Maple
      Dressing, 46–47
Wheatberries, Raisins, and
    Swiss Chard, Creamy
    Orzo with, 100
White Bean Tzatziki Dip, 34
Whole-food, plant-based,
    and SOS-free
    (WFPBSOS) diets, 3
Whole-food, plant-based
    (WFPB) diets, 3
Worcestershire Sauce,
    Plant-Based, 139

Z

Zucchini
  Curried Zucchini Soup, 63
  Ratatouille, 102

ACKNOWLEDGMENTS

First and foremost, I would like to thank my family for putting up with three slow cookers out on the counters for the past four months and for taste-testing every recipe in this book, whether they were your favorite ingredients or not.

Next, I want to thank my editor, Gleni Bartels, without whom some of these recipes might never have been developed (stuffing, anyone?). Thank you for your organization, your editing mastery, and your collaborative spirit.

Thank you to my plant-based friends, especially Kathleen Gage of the *Plant-Based Eating for Health* podcast and Brian Rodgers, the father of plant-based BBQ. I am grateful for your encouragement and your support. I also want to thank Dr. Arianna Coe for suggesting that I try plant-based eating to lower my cholesterol and flatten my bulging belly. It worked.

Thank you to the plant-based authors, bloggers, doctors, and documentarians who put so much time and effort into creating useful information that helps countless people discover and live their healthiest lives.

Finally, I thank the members of my Plant-Based Home Cooking with Felicia Slattery Facebook group for your excitement, energy, and enthusiasm as I developed and launched this book and my brand. Without you asking for my recipes, I might never have walked this path or written these words.

ABOUT THE AUTHOR

Felicia Slattery is an award-winning home cook who began her adventures in the kitchen at a young age. In high school she took every cooking class offered, worked in restaurants through high school and college (and beyond), took cooking classes in Paris, France, at Le Cordon Bleu, and is now a popular food blogger. She is the creator of PlantBasedHomeCooking.com and the Facebook group and YouTube channel Plant Based Home Cooking with Felicia Slattery, where she regularly shares her recipes and stories and helps others discover the joy of living a healthy, plant-based lifestyle.

Printed in the USA
CPSIA information can be obtained
at www.ICGtesting.com
LVHW082042040124
767685LV00004B/24